ONCE AROUND *the* SUN

"*Once Around the Sun* is a delightful family treasure. Cultures throughout the world have used storytelling as a way to pass on knowledge, and this book's stories and poems alone make it worth owning. Yet, its recipes and activities add another dimension that makes this book an invaluable resource for parents wanting to share ancient cultures and beliefs with their children. Young ones are sure to love activities such as making a magic wand and writing secret rune messages with invisible ink. I would highly recommend this fun and informative book for any family that wishes to explore the seasonal stories and celebrations."

ROBIN CORAK, AUTHOR OF *PERSEPHONE*:
PRACTICING THE ART OF PERSONAL POWER

"Ellen Evert Hopman has written a book that will delight children, families, and those who are looking for traditions to explore and stories to share as they celebrate the holidays. I especially love the tales that beg to be read aloud and, as with all good folk stories, add depth and ancient wisdom with the telling. Recipes and special crafts to make with children meaningfully connect folk customs with the seasonal changes. *Once Around the Sun* is a book not only enjoyed with the first reading but also when it is picked up and read again and again with each turn of the seasonal wheel."

LAURA WILDMAN-HANLON, AUTHOR OF *WHAT'S YOUR WICCA IQ?*,
WICCAN MEDITATIONS, AND *CELEBRATING THE PAGAN SOUL*

"For all of us, children and adults, who love fairy and folk stories, these nine tales told by Ellen Evert Hopman carry us to the roots of ancient lore. Earth, sky, and the waters are embodied in Gods and Goddesses with power to bring feast or famine, health or disease, tragedy or happiness, depending on their actions—and the hard work, gratitude, and faithfulness of humans. Alongside the stories are embedded recipes, games, and verse. This book is a treasure trove for curious children and their grown-ups, who wish to bring the rich spirits of the natural world to life."

PATRICIA LEE LEWIS, AUTHOR OF *A KIND OF YELLOW*

"*Once Around the Sun* is a welcome addition to the growing body of literature written for children and their parents. Hopman uses the structure of 'wheel of the year' to explore the meanings and celebrations of each season through a selection of stories from a variety of countries and traditions. With its beautiful illustrations from artist Lauren A. Mills, this book is sure to be enjoyed by children of all ages."

FIONA TINKER, AUTHOR OF *STORIES FOR THE SONGS OF THE YEAR* AND CONTRIBUTOR TO *POOKA PAGES MAGAZINE FOR PAGAN KIDS*

"Now we can all share the glory of seasonal celebration with our children and grandchildren, so they can sweep out the old year with La Befana, make runes like a Viking, knead soda bread for Imbolg, and drink the herbal teas of the season. All the traditional stories, songs, and celebrations take the family through the year with joy and blessing."

CAITLÍN MATTHEWS, COAUTHOR OF *THE LOST BOOK OF THE GRAIL* AND AUTHOR OF *THE ART OF CELTIC SEERSHIP*

"From the Cailleach to La Befana, this skillful storyteller—this blessed shanachie—weaves a splendid wreath to revel in the seasons of the rolling year. Beautiful illustrations, recipes, and an inspiring foreword by Jane Yolen envelop this tender reminder of the importance of myth and story in making us healthy, happy human beings. A must-have for your bedside reading stack!"

H. BYRON BALLARD, AUTHOR OF *SEASONS OF A MAGICAL LIFE* AND *ROOTS, BRANCHES, AND SPIRITS*

"The traditions, rituals, and stories of the eight celebrations of the wheel of light are full of beautiful energy—stories that bring to life the spirits of the Earth, spirits that many may call fantasy, but I know differently. *Once Around the Sun* brings to life that which comes from beyond our senses with the traditions and rituals of reaching out and giving back to the spirits and fairies with food and other gifts."

NICHOLAS E. BRINK, PH.D., AUTHOR OF *BALDR'S MAGIC*

ONCE AROUND *the* SUN

Stories, Crafts, and Recipes to Celebrate the Sacred Earth Year

ELLEN EVERT HOPMAN

ILLUSTRATED BY LAUREN MILLS

Destiny Books
Rochester, Vermont

Destiny Books
One Park Street
Rochester, Vermont 05767
www.DestinyBooks.com

Destiny Books is a division of Inner Traditions International

Cataloging-in-Publication Data for this title is available from the Library of Congress

ISBN 978-1-64411-414-8 (print)
ISBN 978-1-64411-415-5 (ebook)

Printed and bound in the United States by Versa Press, Inc.

10   9   8   7   6   5   4   3   2   1

Text design and layout by Virginia Scott Bowman
This book was typeset in Garamond Premier Pro, Frutiger, and Gill Sans with Trajan Pro
and Belda used as the display typefaces

To send correspondence to the author of this book, mail a first-class letter to the
author c/o Inner Traditions • Bear & Company, One Park Street, Rochester, VT 05767,
and we will forward the communication, or contact the author directly at
www.elleneverthopman.com. To send correspondence to the illustrator of this book,
follow the above or contact the illustrator directly at **laurenmillsart.com**.

CONTENTS

Thanks are due to Andrew Theitic for his memories of an Italian Christmas and La Befana, and to Dr. Jane Sibley for advice on Norse matters. Thanks are also due to Lauren A. Mills for her helpful comments on the stories. My gratitude goes to Sharynne MacLeod NicMhacha for advice on Gaelic wording and to Tara Tine, Irish witch and YouTuber, for correcting my fledgling Irish. And a special thanks to Seanán Mac Aoidh, who helped me sort the Old Irish from the Modern Irish. Any mistakes are my own.

Much appreciation goes to Lauren A. Mills for the gorgeous illustrations, and my eternal gratitude to Jane Yolen for the inspiring foreword.

STORIES THAT BRING THE SUN UP

Jane Yolen

In these dark days, ringed with disease, disasters, disinterest, and disinformation, author Ellen Evert Hopman reminds us: "What withers away into blackness will be born again once the Sun rises."

To prove this, she hands us a canticle of nine Old European folktales to mark the festival seasons. Here we have the past informing the present. These stories are in touch with both old and new traditions, and she makes the most of every single one.

Hopman is not just handing us fairy-tale wisdom, not just telling stories borne on gossamer wings. Rather, she has given us the deep murmurations and incantations of the world—of hope, belief, faith, love.

I, too, have spent a long lifetime poking into the past, learning the tales about the little folk and big folk, soaking up the old stories and ballads. I have come under their spell many times. It is both a tangle and a wide walkway, both a maze and an amazement, filled with myth, magic, mayhem. And the sunrise.

Hopman's stories in this book come from Ireland, Scotland, Poland, Italy, Germany. There's a tale from the Anglo-Saxons (the early English) and even an American version of an Orkney (Scottish) one. And if that were all she showcased here, I would still feel the *blessed-be* of the Goddess worshippers.

But Hopman has not stopped there. Additionally, she has given us guides—pronunciations, histories, explanations. There are, as well, some old recipes to accompany various stories—from a full tea to a nettle soup to bannocks, bilberry pie, and gingerbread loaf. There are lovely projects for children to make, each one special to the holiday story—a magic wand, a magic broom, dolls, games, rag trees, Easter egg dye, Maypoles, and more.

And all this is accompanied by information about the sacredness and magic of nature, herbal remedies, the making and reading of runes . . .

In other words, this book is a cornucopia of medicines, magics, and marvels of our world. There are stories here for adults and children, projects for all ages, new (old) words to learn, new (old) ideas to explore.

To top it all off, one of the finest living American fairy-tale illustrators—artist Lauren Mills—has done the paintings throughout. I have known her work for years, and she always surprises and delights.

So, whether you read this book for information, for direction, out of curiosity, or for delight, and whether you will be learning some of these things for the first time or perhaps are once again amazed at how powerful and rich folk cultures once were, I know you will remember that the past informs the present. I know you will remember that we become our better selves by acknowledging that, and not giving in to despair at the current state of things. Most important, I know you will remember that what withers away into blackness will be born again once the Sun rises.

At least in these difficult days, that is our hope and our prayer—and the promise that the old folk cultures give.

JANE YOLEN is the author of more than 400 books ranging from fantasy to science fiction to children's books. Her books have won numerous awards including the Caldecott Medal, two Nebula Awards, and three World Fantasy Awards. She has also won the World Fantasy Association's Lifetime Achievement Award. Among her beloved books are *Favorite Folktales from Around the World, Fairy Tale Feasts, Jewish Fairy Tale Feasts, Gray Heroes: Elder Tales from Around the World,* and *How to Fracture a Fairy Tale.* She divides her time between Western Massachusetts; Mystic, Connecticut; and Scotland.

INTRODUCTION

THE CIRCLE
WILL GO 'ROUND

MY MESSAGE TO PARENTS AND TEACHERS

I have been an adherent of nature-based religions for more than thirty years now. During that time, I have watched species disappear, the climate change, and civilization-altering events, such as wars, famines, and pandemics, take place. The one unchanging source of comfort and support for me has always been Great Nature. In the spring, I look forward to the first crocuses and violets. In summer, I can count on the hummingbirds and roses to appear. In the fall, I watch as the maples turn their glowing colors and I collect acorns to make flour. In winter, I delight in the snow and cozy, quiet days of writing in the warm kitchen.

Our forebearers were closer to these kinds of Earth changes because they were not distracted by smartphones, computers, and television. They honored the stations of the Earth year with song, tales told by the fire, and seasonal feasts. It is my hope that this volume will be a guide to the Earth festivals for parents, teachers, and children, providing tales, recipes, and crafts that evoke a slower, more Earth-conscious time. May it pass on to the future the awareness of all the unseen spirits that shape our world and influence our lives, and may it illuminate the sacred within every leaf and flower.

TO THE KIDS WHO READ THIS BOOK

Please read these stories out loud! Read them to your parents, grandparents, brothers, and sisters. If you don't have siblings, then consider reading them to your pets! Look at the date given for each story. Read the winter tales in winter and the summer tales in summer. Make a craft to go along with each story, and cook a dish that celebrates the season. Ask your family to help you, and make it a celebration that inspires all your senses—touch, taste, sight, hearing, smell, and imagination!

A LITTLE MORE ABOUT HONORING
NATURE AND THE SEASONS

I want to share this lovely little tale from Kansas City storyteller, poet, Druid, and photographer Shawn Moore because it speaks so beautifully of nature spirituality, which is my own chosen path. This experience came to him while he was meditating and listening to Celtic music.

At first, I find myself in my garden, enjoying that peace and oneness I always feel when I have my hands in the soil, planting a seedling I've grown and cared for over the past month.

Then there's a gray fogginess to my vision.

I find myself in a field, and I'm holding on to a plow being pulled by an ox. Looking around, I see a woman and children playing by a roundhouse at the other end of the field. Maybe it's a family I have forgotten through time, or maybe the family I still have, just in a past life.

I barely have a moment to look down at my feet before I take flight over a hill and through the mist until I find myself in a deep forest.

I hear soft flute music, and I follow it until I see a beautiful young maiden playing in a ray of sunshine shining through a hole in the forest canopy.

This young flute player is surrounded by different types of animals, birds, and insects, with more and more coming toward her, all in a huge circle, the larger animals letting the smaller ones ride upon their backs and antlers to gain a better view.

Alas, I understand this is no maiden. This is the Mother Goddess herself. She's not playing a melody for the Earth's creatures; she's speaking to them through the music.

I realize then that the notes of the flute are teardrops upon her face, and there is sadness in her heart.

She asks the animals, "Why do they not listen? Why do they not see?"

The animals do not answer in language, but I understand their words.

"We don't know, Mother. We've tried to warn them, but they no longer understand our speech."

The Mother Goddess answers, "How could I have let this go so far? For ages I have watched them plunder and destroy, but I always had hope that one day they would learn, and then heal. I fear it may be too late."

At this, a great sadness overtakes all the animals, and the Mother Goddess knows it. Her melody changes from solemn to cheerful, and she says, "Do not be sad, my children, all is not lost. Like all things, even I may have to darken and wither until everything is gone. But as it has been since the beginning and through all the ages, what withers away into blackness will be born again once the Sun rises. This is how it has always been, this is the way it is now, and this is the way for eternity. The circle will go 'round, and all that is lost shall be again!"

I then return to my body.

I felt I needed to put this story down and am sharing it with all of you.

Shawn's lovely vision perfectly describes the round of the seasons and the circle of life. Which is exactly what this book is all about!

THE HOLIDAYS OF
THE SACRED EARTH YEAR

All the festivals described in this book are ones that my friends and I observe. We are followers of the Earth religion, also known as Nature Spirituality. We consider the Earth and her creatures to be our sacred responsibility, and we try to protect the land as best we can. We do this by recycling, buying used clothes and furniture, driving less, and paying

*The author celebrating
the Sacred Earth*

attention to the way our food and other things we buy are grown and packaged. When we celebrate together, we give thanks to the Earth, to our ancestors who worked hard so we can be alive today, and to the unseen Faeries, angels, and spirits who help our gardens grow.

This book begins with the Celtic Samhain festival, now known as Halloween, because the Celtic year traditionally began at that time. By Samhain all the produce of the fields had to be safely stowed away and the animals housed snuggly in the barn. Samhain marked the final end of the harvest of the previous year, it was a dark time and the beginning of the coldest weather. Now the focus of the farm moved inside, to indoor crafts and skills. During these indoor days storytellers appeared at the gates to spin tales by the fire.

The ancient Celts also calculated days this way: each day began at sunset, echoing the idea that all things have their beginnings in the dark.

If you think about it, all life emerges from darkness. A seed deep under the soil, a baby animal growing in its mother's belly, all start in the dark. Even space, the place from which our solar system and galaxy were born, is mostly dark.

The next festival, Winter Solstice, marks the darkest day of all and the longest night. After that the light gradually returns and keeps growing steadily until high summer. Then the descent into the dark starts all over again!

A TALE OF THE CAILLEACH, THE GREAT GODDESS OF WINTER

An Irish Tale for Samhain
(October 31–November 1)

Gods, Goddesses, Spirits, and Magical Beings:

Cailleach (*KAHL-yuk*)—a Goddess of the land and in some areas the Goddess of winter.

Irish/Gaelic Words to Know:

Beltaine (*BELL-tayn*)—the Celtic May Day festival, when herds of animals (like cows and sheep) were ritually blessed by having them pass between two great fires on their way up to their summer pasture in the hills. The traditional Irish spelling is Bealtaine *(be-OWL-tin-eh)*.

Eanáir (*AHN-oar*)—January.

Imbolg (*IH-molg*)—a Celtic festival held on February 1–2 celebrating the lactation of ewes, who give birth at about this time, and the Goddess Brighid. A medieval name for the festival is Oimelc, "ewe's milk."

Samhain (*SOH-win*)—a holiday, celebrated from October 31 to November 1, marking the date by which all produce from the fields had to be safely harvested and stored, because anything left out after that time belonged to the Faeries. In modern times, we call this celebration Halloween.

> **shanachie (*SHAH-na-key*)**—a traditional teller of tales;
> sometimes spelled *seanchaí*.
> **slaitín draíochta (*SLAY-tin DRAY-och-ta*)**—a magic wand.

. . . .

For the ancient Celts, there were only two seasons of the year: winter and summer. Winter began at Samhain, and summer began at Beltaine. In those days, when homes were lit only by candles and people traveled on foot or by horse, wintertime could be dark and dreary. So, after dinner, the family would wash and dry the dishes and then sit down before the hearth to hear a story. Sometimes storytellers called *shanachies* would visit from house to house and, in exchange for a meal, offer a tale or two. In this way, the long, cold nights were made warm and cozy as the elders passed their history and traditions down to the children, just as the geese teach their young to fly south each year.

✳

The old shanachie had been visiting the snug little thatched cottage where Fiona lived since before she was born. On Samhain Eve, he appeared as usual to tell the story of the Cailleach, the great Goddess of Winter, whom some called the Bone Mother or the Great Hag, for on that very night her reign was beginning and the whole family was gathered to learn and remember.

After they'd eaten and the family had gathered in front of the fire, the shanachie began his tale. "Tonight, the world is turning from the season of meadow larks and bees, of apples and grain and flowers, to the quiet days of frost and snow," he said. He was looking Fiona in the eye, because she was the youngest member of the family and he wanted to make sure she took in every word. "Now begins the time of cold, darkness, and death. Your father, brothers, and uncles have gathered the flocks and bolted them into their snug pen. Your mother, aunts, and sisters have ground the sausages, salted the meat, and hidden the apples in their straw-lined pit. The grain is safely stored, dry and clean in sacks in the barn. Outside the wind is singing a song of coming storms. The Great Hag of Winter is on the move!"

The shanachie paused for effect, taking a slow drink from a cup of herbal tea that Fiona's grandmother had thoughtfully placed beside his chair.

"How does the Goddess travel?" Fiona asked.

The shanachie replied, "She travels on the back of a wolf. That is why many people call Eanáir, the coldest month of the year, the Wolf Month."

"Is she the one who makes the ice and snow?" asked Fiona.

"Oh yes, that is one of her greatest powers," said the shanachie, smiling.

"How ever does she do that?" asked Fiona. Her eyes were as wide and round as the Moon in the sky.

"Well," said the shanachie, "in the west of Scotland, in the ocean, is the giant whirlpool of Corryvreckan. That place is the Cailleach's wash-tub. Every year at Samhain she scrubs her plaids in that whirlpool, and they come out as white as frost. After that, the land is covered in snow because, you see, her plaids are the land itself."

"But doesn't she do her washing at any other time?" asked Fiona, because it seemed strange to do laundry only once a year.

"Oh yes, indeed," said the shanachie. "When the whirlpool is filled with foam, that means she is treading her laundry by trampling it with her feet. And if you hear a loud clap of thunder, that means she is sneezing!"

That remark provoked giggles from the whole family.

The shanachie continued, "You see, the Ancient Veiled One is so tall that she can easily wade across lakes and rivers, and she likes to leap from hilltop to hilltop. She carries a wicker basket filled with stones on her back, and wherever she drops a stone, an island or a mountain forms. She also carries a *slaitín draíochta* made of aspen wood to blast away any small scrap of green that dares to poke up its head in the dark season. And wherever she touches the ground with her wand, the soil instantly freezes as hard as stone!"

Fiona shivered and snuggled deeper into her mother's lap.

"Her reign ends at Beltaine, when she hides her slaitín draíochta in a spiky thicket of holly or a bristly tangle of gorse. She picks it up when the year turns to winter once again."

"But what does she do all summer?" asked Fiona. "Six months is an awfully long time to wait, with nothing to do."

"Oh, she is still busy," replied the shanachie. "The Ancient One has plenty of work all year. You see, she likes to roam the countryside with her cows and goats and lead them to the beach to eat seaweed. As she is the Goddess of the Land, she loves all animals. She is also the guardian of the deer and makes sure they stay happy and healthy.

"Even though they can't see her," he continued, "she whispers thoughts into the hunter's ears, advising them how many deer to shoot and at which times. Good hunters show her every respect because she reminds them to always honor the balance of nature. The best hunters will always bless the animals they have taken to feed their family, because they know that if they forget to do that, the meat will belong to the Faeries. And they will always remember to whisper thanks to the Goddess for her generous bounty."

Fiona had never seen a Faery, though she could sometimes hear them singing when she sat very still in the forest. "How do the Faeries get the meat if the hunter forgets to bless it?" she asked.

"Ah, a good question, and here's a tale to remember," the shanachie replied. "One time some boys went out and shot a deer. They were very excited and proud of themselves, imagining all the praise they would get when they returned to their village. They completely forgot to bless the meat or to thank the deer that had given its life. All they did was tie a rope around the deer's legs and begin to drag it home."

"When they got back to their village, even though they had felt the heavy weight of the deer the whole way through the forest, all they had was an empty rope dragging behind them. The deer had disappeared! You see, the Faeries took it, to teach them a lesson."

"How can there be only an empty rope if they still felt the weight of the deer?" Fiona asked, crossing her arms and shaking her head in disbelief.

The shanachie smiled, taking another sip of the excellent herbal tea.

"Ah, sure, you haven't yet come across Faery magic, but your grandmother has. It's in this tea that surely the Faeries have blessed."

Fiona's grandmother smiled with a nod, and the shanachie continued.

"Now, the Cailleach is a woman of magic and mystery, too. Sometimes she appears as a seagull. She may also appear as an eagle, a heron, or a cormorant. When she and her helpers ride on the backs of wolves or wild pigs, they are often followed by herds of deer or wild boar.

"In the season of summer, she sometimes shape-shifts into a large stone," he told her, holding his hands out wide to show her just how big. "You will know which one because it is always wet, even in the driest season. At Imbolg, she gathers firewood to last her until Beltaine. If the weather is good and she can collect a great store of wood to warm the house, that means there is still a long winter ahead. But if the weather is drizzly and cloudy and she is forced to stay inside, that means the winter is nearly over.

"The Ancient Veiled One can bless or curse the tribes, depending on whether they honor her properly," he continued. "We should always remember to thank her because she is the one who taught the people how to thresh the grain, using a flail made of holly wood with a striker made of hazel.* She also taught us to thresh on a clean floor, to sow oats in late winter, and to harvest the green grain before the late summer storms set in."

"Does she ever come to our farm?" Fiona asked. "How will I know if she has been here?"

"Well," said the shanachie, "if you have ever seen a pile of stones or a solitary boulder at the top of a mountain, that is a spot that is sacred to her. It is proper to leave a gift of oatcakes or butter at such a place. There are stones like that nearby; I am sure you have seen them while you were out picking berries. A solitary stone standing in the landscape can be a sign of her presence, too. That is often a person or animal she turned to stone because they didn't show her the proper respect."

---

*A *flail* is a threshing tool made of a wooden staff with a short heavy stick swinging from it.

Fiona gulped.

"Mountain springs are her special sanctuaries, and she drinks from them to renew her powers. If you find a hidden forest spring, you should walk around it nine times and then drink from its waters. Be sure to leave an offering of thanks, too; a bit of cheese or bread and some cider or honey are nice. But if you don't have those with you, you can always offer a prayer or a song.

"And now," he said, getting up from his seat by the fire, "you know all about the Cailleach, the ancient Bone Mother and sacred Goddess of the Land. I hope you will show her every honor in the coming season of snow and ice."

And with that, he put on his warm cloak, winked at Fiona, and disappeared out the door into the windy, wild weather.

🌿 FIONA'S GRANDMOTHER'S WINTERTIME TEA 🌿

Dried lavender flowers

Dried nettle leaves

Oatstraw

Dried raspberry leaves

Dried rose petals

Dried elderberries

Dried rose hips

Fresh white pine needles, optional

Chopped dried apples

Raw honey

Measure out equal amounts of the lavender flowers, nettle leaves, oatstraw, raspberry leaves, and rose petals. Mix them together.

To make a single cup of tea, combine 1 cup of water with 1 teaspoon of elderberries and 1 teaspoon of rose hips in a pan. (Add 1 teaspoon of chopped fresh white pine needles from the forest if you are using the tea for healing purposes. They taste lemony and have more vitamin C than lemons!)

Bring to a boil, then reduce the heat, cover, and let simmer for 20 minutes.

Remove the pan from the stove. Add 1 teaspoon of the herb mix you made earlier, along with 1 teaspoon chopped dried apples.

Cover and let steep for another 20 minutes

Strain out the herbs and apples. Add honey to taste and serve.

🦊 COLCANNON: 🍂
A POTATO DISH FOR SAMHAIN

Fall is the time to gather root vegetables such as carrots, turnips, rutaba-gas, and potatoes. Here is a traditional recipe for colcannon, an Irish potato dish that's perfect for a Samhain celebration. For this and for all the recipes in this book, I hope you will use the best-quality ingredients possible, like locally grown and organic!

> 4 large potatoes, peeled and cut into chunks
>
> Sea salt
>
> 6 tablespoons butter, plus extra for serving
>
> 3 cups chopped cabbage, chard, or kale
>
> ½ cup minced green onions (scallions)
>
> 1 cup milk (cow, soy, almond, cashew, coconut, rice, oat, hemp, or flax), half-and-half, or cream

Place the potatoes in a large pot and add enough water to cover them by a couple of inches.

Add a pinch of sea salt.

Boil the potatoes until they are tender enough to pierce with a fork, then drain them.

In a separate pot, melt the butter over medium-high heat. Add the chopped greens and sauté until they are wilted.

Fold in the green onions and cook for 1 minute longer.

Mash the potatoes with the milk.

Mix the mashed potatoes into the greens.

Season to taste with salt and serve hot, with a large lump of butter in the middle of the dish.

To eat, take a forkful of potatoes and greens and dip it into the butter.

_____

This recipe is adapted from Elise Bauer, "Colcannon," Simply Recipes (website), March 12, 2019; updated June 23, 2021.

_____ ❋ _____

Make Your Own Magic Wand

The Cailleach has a slaitín draíochta (magic wand) of great power that she uses to control the weather. You can make your own magic wand from wood that you find. It's always more powerful to make your own magical tool, rather than buying one in a store. When you put your personal energy into your magical tools, they respond more strongly to your wishes and intentions.

➤➤ Go outside, to your backyard or to the woods, especially after a big storm. Look for a branch that has fallen to the ground. That kind of wood is a gift freely given by the trees for your use. When you find the correct piece of wood, it will feel "right" in your hand. Don't worry if it's a little bent or crooked—that just makes it more unique!

➤➤ Leave a small gift of thanks, like some herbs, a bit of honey, milk or cider, a prayer, or a song, to thank the trees for their help.

➤➤ When you get home, you can peel the bark off the wood if you like, or just leave it in place if that feels right to you.

➤➤ Light a candle and let it burn for a while, then tip it slightly on its side over a dish and let it drip until a small puddle of wax has formed. Dip both ends of your wand into the pool of wax to coat them. The wax seals the ends of the wood so it won't dry out too quickly (to prevent splitting).

➤➤ If you feel extra inspired, you can carve symbols and letters into your wand. Or you can just leave it plain.

Once you have your wand, sit very still with your eyes closed and ask it if it has a name. You can also ask it what kind of magic it carries and how it wants to be used. Your wand may change over time and have different names and purposes.

To use your wand, feel your intention as strongly as you can. Holding that thought in your mind, point your wand toward an altar or a sacred object, such as a special stone or crystal. Visualize a stream of light going from the tip of your wand to your altar or object and, from there, out to the world.

When you are not using it, wrap your wand in a cloth or store it in its own bag.

The kind of wood you choose for your wand is important because the particular personality of the tree will help to amplify your magic. On the next page is a list of some of the trees whose wood you might find and a little bit about their qualities.

Magic wands!
Photo by Nathan MacTaggart.

Apple: love magic, traveling to the land of the Faeries (and back!)

Ash: communication with the three worlds (land, sea, and sky), mastery, leadership

Birch: new beginnings, communication with Goddesses

Cedar: peace, cleansing, healing, preparation for prayer

Cherry: beauty contests, quests for beauty, competitions of all kinds

Chestnut: love, warding off illness, good luck, prosperity

Elder: healing, communication with Mother Earth and forest spirits

Elm: communication with the Elves, soothing of pain

Eucalyptus: cleansing, purification, protection, warding off illness and negativity

Hawthorn: communication with the Faery realm, May Day magic, healing the heart

Hazel: wisdom, scholarship, and learning

Holly: warrior spirit, strength in battle, overcoming difficulties and obstacles

Larch: sacred groves, healing wounds (both physical and spiritual)

Maple: sweetness and friendship, artistic inspiration

Oak: strength, endurance, communication with the High Gods, finding balance

Pine: rebirth, immortality, flexibility, cleansing, creating peace

Poplar: communication with the spirits of air, sending messages

Rowan (Mountain Ash): magical protection, healing

Walnut: breaking spells, easing transitions, healing brain injuries

Willow: poetry, gentleness, healing touch, the Moon

You can read many more details about the magic and lore of trees and learn to use them for food and medicine in two of my other books: *A Druid's Herbal of Sacred Tree Medicine* (2008) and *Tree Medicine, Tree Magic* (second edition, 2017).

OLD NISSE AND THE RETURN OF SUNNA, THE SUN GODDESS

A Norse Tale for Yule and the Winter Solstice (December 20/21/22/23)

·············· **Key Figures and Terms** ··············

Gods, Goddesses, Spirits, and Magical Beings:

Frey (*fray*)—a God of peace, fertility, rain, and sunshine. Brother to Freya.

Freya (*FRAY-uh*)—a Goddess of love, beauty, sex, fertility, gold, and sometimes war and death. Sister to Frey.

Nisser (*NIH-sehr*)—solitary, mischievous domestic sprites and gnomes responsible for the protection and welfare of the farmstead and its out buildings. The singular form of the word is *Nisse*.

Sköll (*Scohl*)—a wolf spirit and pursuer of the Sun.

Sunna (*SOON-ah*)—the Sun Goddess. She was once human and rose to the rank of Goddess by the intervention of the Gods. Sister to the Moon God, Manni.

Thor (*thoar*)—a hammer-wielding God of thunder, lightning, storms, oak trees, strength, protection of humanity, hallowing (honoring as sacred), and fertility. Thor rides the

19

sky in a chariot drawn by two white goats, distributing gifts around the time of the Winter Solstice. It's possible he is the same person who we now call Santa Claus.

Norse Words to Know:

fadir (*FAH-deer*)—father.

modir (*MOH-deer*)—mother.

Ragnarök (*RAG-nah-rock*)—a terrible battle between the forces of good and evil at the end of the world.

Yggdrasil (*IG-drah-sill*)—the cosmic ash tree at the geographical center of the Norse spiritual world. It represents the cycle of birth, growth, death, and rebirth.

. . . .

Yuletide is an old word for what many of us now call the Christmas season. It comes from the Old Norse words *jul* (pronounced *yul*) or *jól* (pronounced *yoh-l*). The Norse Vikings were traders and raiders who had a Lunar calendar. Their Jólablót (*YOH-lah-bloht*), a midwinter festival associated with the rebirth of the Sun, was celebrated on the first full Moon following the first new Moon past the Winter Solstice. The celebration began with Mōdraniht (*MOH-drah-need*), Night of the Mothers or Mothers' Night, a Goddess-honoring festival at sunset of the Winter Solstice.

They also had a Yuletide figure called Yule Fadir, who was most likely who we now call Father Christmas (or Santa Claus). Some say that Yule Fadir was really the long-bearded God Odin (*OH-din*), who sometimes bears the name Jólnir (*YOHL-neer,* the Yule one).

✳

Bjorn and Astrid were the children of Vikings who lived in a sod house,* nestled in the hills of Norway, not far from the sea. When Fadir, their

---

*A sod house in Viking times usually had two rows of thick wooden pillars that held up the thatched roof, benches along the walls to sit and sleep on, and a long central fire pit where the cooking was done.

father, went on trading trips in his boat, Modir, their mother, stayed home to weave textiles on her loom and to tend the fields and animals.

Bjorn and Astrid helped with the many chores that needed to be done, such as cooking and washing, carding wool, keeping the hearth fire going, cleaning the barn, and tending to the goats and chickens. When Fadir was away, they were sent to the barn at dusk to leave an offering of milk and bread for Old Nisse, the elf on the farm who looked after the animals at night. Astrid, who was younger than her brother, Bjorn, was the only one in the family who could see and hear the elf. Old Nisse enjoyed the little girl's company, especially her singing, and so he often helped her gather sticks for the hearth fire.

It was early fall and the weather was good, so Fadir was preparing to sail away on a trading trip, the last one of the year. As he left, he said to the children, "I will be back before the snow falls and in time for Yule. While I'm away, you must not forget Old Nisse. If he is ignored, he could make our butter and milk turn bad or bring bad luck to the farm!"

Astrid took in the words, but Bjorn hardly listened. He thought making offerings to a Nisse was just a silly old superstition.

Every day it grew darker and darker until Astrid, Bjorn, and Modir had to carry a lamp to the barn to take care of the goats and chickens. While Modir tended the hens, Astrid poured fresh goat's milk into a bowl for Old Nisse. Bjorn exclaimed, "What a waste! It's either the cats or the rats that are drinking the milk. I may as well drink it myself!"

"No! Bjorn, don't!" Astrid yelled. But it was too late. Bjorn had slurped the milk down in one big gulp.

No sooner had he finished than Old Nisse jumped down from the rafters above and pinched Bjorn's ear.

"Ouch! Astrid, how dare you!" Bjorn cried out, and he reached to pull Astrid's braid, but Old Nisse tripped him from behind. Suddenly Bjorn knew his sister was not the culprit. Now he was afraid. He let Astrid pour another bowlful of milk for Old Nisse and didn't say a word.

The snow began to fall and still Fadir had not returned. Ulf, the children's uncle, would sometimes ski over to their farm and take the children ice skating with their cousins. He hoped it would keep Astrid and Bjorn from worrying about their father.

Ulf would show the children the huge piece of oak he and Fadir had stored in the barn to dry with the other firewood. "You see the runes* we carved into this great log? They are for protection and good luck in the coming year, just as we did last year. Your fadir will soon return."

"But tomorrow begins the twelve days of Yule, and we are supposed to start burning the log. How will you drag it in without Fadir?" Bjorn asked.

"Halfdan, your other uncle, will come tomorrow and we will drag it in together, along with a Yule evergreen to honor the Sun, Sunna," Ulf replied. But Bjorn and Astrid still looked worried.

"What if Fadir's boat has overturned? What if he has been attacked by a wild boar?" Bjorn asked.

"Come with me," said Ulf. "There is something I want to show you."

Ulf brought them to the shed and opened the door, revealing the carcass of a wild boar, frozen solid and hanging inside. "At the last full Moon, your fadir and I killed this wild boar. We brought it back to sacrifice to Frey and Freya so we could get a good crop in the new year. You see, we have ensured good luck and good favor with the Gods, and you have been good to your house elf, I am sure."

Bjorn looked down sheepishly, and Astrid thought her brother might cry. She spoke up. "Old Nisse has not missed a night of milk, and I sing to him every day."

"Then all will be well, but it is still up to the Gods. Tomorrow will be the Winter Solstice. Your aunts and uncles will come, and you will celebrate Yule with your family," said Ulf.

That evening, Bjorn had a bellyache, and so he stayed inside and sipped chamomile and mint tea by the hearth while Astrid went out to the barn to talk with Old Nisse. She called to him by his secret name, which only she knew. Old Nisse sat in the hay with Astrid while she told him her

---

*Viking runes are the letters of the Younger Futhark alphabet (see page 31).

worries about their missing father. He nodded and twirled his long white beard. At last, he replied, "I will call to the owls and to the elves of the forest, and we will all look for Fadir. Now go to bed tonight and dream sweet dreams."

Astrid stood and smiled, and she gave Old Nisse some bread and cheese she had saved in her pocket from her last meal.

He took the gifts with thanks and bowed. "Your brother was right, you know. I don't eat the gifts, but I do enjoy their essence and the thought behind them, and then I gift them to the animals in need."

Astrid kissed the little elf on top of his red cap and skipped back to the house on top of the deep, crusty snow, which carried her weight as if she were as light as a feather.

"Do not worry, Bjorn," she whispered to her brother that night when they were tucked into bed. "Old Nisse is going to look for Fadir with the help of his friends."

Bjorn nodded weakly. "Let's hope the Trolls haven't taken Fadir for what I have done."

The wind howled outside, and Bjorn burrowed beneath the animal skins on his bed. That night, he dreamed that Thor did not bring any gifts. He heard him say, "Because of your naughtiness, Sunna, our Sun, will be swallowed up by the wolf, and only darkness will prevail!"

But Astrid dreamed of Thor riding across the sky in his chariot, pulled by goats and making the sound of thunder as he passed. In his chariot was Old Nisse, peering down at the forest and fields below for Fadir, while Sunna was giving birth to a new Sun.

The next day was the Winter Solstice, and Bjorn was still moping. Modir said, "Bjorn, we must have hope and still celebrate Yule, the longest night of the year, which begins tonight. Your aunts and uncles will come, and your cousins Erik, Revna, Frida, and Leif. There will be stories and poetry, and Aunt Eida will bring her honey cakes and buttermilk, and we will all sing!"

"How can we sing without Fadir? How can we celebrate if we don't know whether he will ever come home?" Bjorn asked dejectedly.

Modir replied, "Fadir will want us to. He will be here in spirit even if he is not here in the flesh." But Modir looked sad and worried, too. "Make sure you keep the fire going," she said to the children. "Even through all the games and feasting, I expect you to keep the Yule log blazing and our dinner cooking. This is the longest night. On this eve, Sunna has been swallowed by the dark wolf Sköll, and she is trapped in the wolf's belly! She is growing weaker and weaker. Even the Gods and Goddesses are feeble and aged now. Their strength, too, is failing. We must keep the fires bright to strengthen Sunna so she can overcome the powers of the dark wolf!"

Astrid and Bjorn went outside to the woodpile and brought in one more armful of sticks and logs to keep the fire going.

Soon Uncle Halfdan and Aunt Thurid arrived, carrying baby Gertrud in a backpack made of skins and fur and dragging in an evergreen tree they'd cut down from the forest behind the house. When they had settled in, Uncle Halfdan helped Ulf bring in the old oak Yule log. Then everyone else arrived and filled the home, making it very crowded indeed.

Halfdan and Thurid rummaged through their backpacks and pulled out tiny beeswax candles, linen-wrapped packets of cookies and honey bread, and little carved images of the Gods. They also had colorful sets of mittens and caps, dyed brightly in red, yellow, and blue by the herbs of the fields and forest.

They handed the objects to everyone. "These are to decorate the Yule tree!" Thurid exclaimed proudly. She had worked hard all year to make the decorations for the Yule festival.

Halfdan set up the evergreen tree they had brought in, tying it to a wooden pillar so it stayed upright, while Thurid handed out small lengths of string and, one by one, everyone took turns tying something to the tree. She was especially proud of the brightness of the wool caps and mittens, which stood out gaily against the dark green of the branches.

Bjorn hardly joined in the fun but only stirred the embers in the fire with the iron tongs.

When the tree was decorated and everyone was relaxed and warm and comfortably seated on the benches, sipping horns and wooden cups full of honey mead, there was a loud pounding on the door.

"Ho, ho, ho!" boomed a deep voice from the starry darkness outside.

Bjorn ran to unbolt the large oaken door, thinking it was Fadir. But it was not. The other children squealed with joy to see Yule Fadir, dressed in a hooded cloak made of goatskins and with a leather mask over his eyes. Astrid and Bjorn tried to smile, and baby Gertrud hid behind her modir's skirt.

"I am Old Man Winter!" the hooded man proclaimed. "I come in the name of Thor, who rides his chariot across the skies and brings gifts for good boys and girls!" Bjorn thought his voice sounded a lot like Frode's, from the farm down the hill, who was the chieftain and spiritual adviser for the community.

Yule Fadir had a huge leather sack on his back. He reached behind to slip it off, opened it, and took out a wooden sword for Erik, a carved and painted spotted cow and a carved bear for Revna and Frida, and a little carved pig for Gertrud to chew on. He handed a small toy ax to Leif, and then bent to pull out a carved wooden doll for Astrid. The little doll had long wooden hair painted yellow, a carved wooden dress colored blue, and a big smile on her face. Astrid thanked Yule Fadir and held the doll tightly to her chest, whispering her dearest wish into the doll's ear.

Then Yule Fadir took out a beautifully carved wooden Viking ship, which he handed to Bjorn. Bjorn loved the ship and thanked him, but he put it to one side, feeling that he did not deserve it. Last, Yule Fadir reached into the sack and brought out wooden spinning tops for each of the children.

Yule Fadir noticed that Bjorn was not playing with his ship, and he pulled him aside. "There is one more gift," he said to Bjorn quietly. "But you must bring it in yourself. Go and open the door."

Puzzled, Bjorn unbolted and swung open the huge door, and to his surprise, another Yule Fadir stood there, wearing a mask and hood. The tall man swooped up Bjorn in his arms, crying, "Ho! Ho! Ho!" as he stamped the snow off his boots.

Astrid and Modir knew for certain whose voice that was, and they ran to hug Fadir.

"This is the best gift of all!" cried Bjorn.

"I tried to come as soon as I could, but ice and snow and darkness overtook me. I have Thor and the last light of Sunna to thank for my safe return." Then, looking at Astrid, Fadir added, "And perhaps I also owe thanks to a particular elf who helped me find my way home."

Astrid and Bjorn settled on Fadir's lap while Yule Fadir bent to his sack one last time. This time he unwrapped a small six-stringed harp and began to sing:

> *Tonight, the old Sun gives birth to her new self.*
> *Elf Shine, Elf Splendor, and Elf Wheel are her names.*
> *With golden hair, and golden eyes, and wearing a*
> *   necklace of fire,*
> *She is the seed of Yggdrasil, the Sacred Ash of the*
> *   Flames.*
> *She is the oldest child and the youngest child of the year.*
> *In the blackness of the wolf's belly, she gives birth to*
> *   herself.*
> *We must send her good thoughts,*
> *good food, and bright lights*
> *to give her strength!*
> *The ancestral mothers are here, too,*
> *the guardians of time and fate,*
> *spinning a new cycle, midwives to the infant Sun!*
> *Mighty Thor is here also,*
> *to shield and protect the newborn Sun*
> *as she reclaims her place in the heavens!*

He continued strumming on his harp as Fadir and Modir began to light the tiny candles the family had tied to the Yule tree. Everyone clapped and smiled as the honey-scented lights perfumed the air and the little lights flickered.

Suddenly, a fierce wind picked up outside the walls of the long house, licking and ruffling through the thatch above like a hungry beast. It even fingered its way down the smoke hole to the fire below, spreading smoke to all the corners of the dwelling.

"Do not be afraid!" said Yule Fadir. "It is but the Wild Hunt. The Yule Riders are wandering the skies. Ghosts and spirits always come out in the darkest season because now the Earth resembles their underworld home." Just as he spoke these words, a rush of icy wind clawed through the walls, making everyone shiver with fear and excitement.

"And now the Nisser, Faeries, and Trolls come to seek their due!" said Yule Fadir. "Be sure to put out an offering for them so they spare the farm and don't spoil the milk and butter!"

"I won't forget!" Bjorn said sincerely.

Modir had set a bowl of porridge with butter on top by the fire to keep warm, and now she handed it to Fadir, along with a cup of buttermilk, and Fadir put on his skins again, to go bravely out into the windy, cold night and leave these offerings in the barn. Bjorn begged to go with him, and Fadir agreed, so Bjorn brought one of his own cookies and another that Astrid had given him for Old Nisse.

When the pair got back from the barn, the boar on the spit was finally roasted to perfection, and it was time for the feast to begin. Modir filled everyone's wooden bowl to the brim, and no more words were heard, only the sounds of slurping and munching and crunching as everyone dug happily into their holiday meal.

At last Yule Fadir spoke. "You have all done well this night. You have eaten and sung, lit the candles and kindled the Yule log. You have sent strength and joy to Sunna in her labor to escape the belly of the wolf Sköll. You must do all this without fail every year, because if you don't and Sköll wins, then Ragnarök, the twilight of the Gods when the world ends, will come.

"But have no fear," he reassured them. "When that happens, the sacred ash tree Yggdrasil will split wide open, and a human male and female will emerge to create a new world of love and peace, where Sunna can shine once more!"

Then he wrapped up his harp and put it into his sack, burping politely a few times to show that he had eaten his fill, and Fadir thanked him and showed him to the door.

Modir reached up to the rafters, pulling down a large, round wreath made of evergreens, and Fadir hung it on a nail in the wall. "This circle of greens is to welcome the round Sun and also the forest spirits, so they feel comfortable in our home," Modir said proudly. The wreath was beautifully made, bound with strands of ivy and decorated with red rose hips and holly berries.

Then Modir reached up to the rafters and took down a spray of mistletoe* that she had hidden there, and she hung it from a roof beam. "This is the most sacred plant of all," she told the children. "It was created when Thor's lightning struck a mighty oak, and it still has some of his magic. It cures all ills!"

The next morning, upon leaving, everyone broke off a piece of the mistletoe as a gift to hang in the rafters of their home all year to bless their household and land. Twelve days later, at the end of the Yule festival, Fadir gave every family member a piece of the burned Yule log to keep in their home as magical protection. And the Sun was already visibly strengthening in the frosty skies!

---

*The mistletoe that the Vikings used for medicine was *Viscum album,* which is different from American mistletoe, *Phoradendron serotinum* (the berries of both species are poisonous and should never be swallowed). Only use mistletoe as medicine with medical supervision!

MAKE VIKING FOODS FOR YOUR YULE SUPPER
······································

Roasted pork is a traditional food to serve at a Viking Yule feast. In ancient times, Vikings would have roasted a whole boar! When the roast, called the "Oath Boar," was brought to the table, each person made a solemn oath to the God Frey. These sacred oaths were taken very seriously and were meant to be kept.

The ancient Norse believed that the God Frey rode on a great boar called Gullinbursti (Golden Bristles), while his sister, Freya, had a boar called Hildisvíni (Battle Swine). Boars were seen as animals of heroic valor and strength.

🌿 ROASTED VEGETABLES, VIKING STYLE 🌿

The ancient Vikings did not have potatoes, but they did have other root vegetables such as turnips and carrots (though their carrots were white, not orange).

> 2 or 3 large carrots, chopped
> 1 turnip, chopped
> Sea salt
> ¼ head cabbage, chopped
> 1 large leek, chopped
> Raw honey

Combine the carrots and turnip in a pot with a bit of sea salt and enough water to cover them by a couple of inches. Bring to a boil, then reduce the heat and simmer for 5 minutes. Drain.

Melt a bit of butter in a large pan over medium heat. (The Vikings never used oil for cooking!) Add the carrots and turnips and sauté until they are soft.

Add the cabbage and leek and sauté until soft.

Sprinkle the vegetables with sea salt and drizzle with honey. Toss well to coat them evenly. Serve warm.

🦌 SALMON PATTIES 🌿

The Vikings loved fish and ate a lot of it, because they lived near the sea. This recipe calls for fresh fillets, but you could substitute two 7-ounce cans of wild salmon; just drain the salmon and use it in place of the cooked salmon.

¾ cup quick-cooking oats

2 (6- to 7-ounce) wild salmon fillets, cooked until they flake easily with a fork

1 egg, beaten

1 tablespoon chopped onion

1 teaspoon chopped fresh (or dried) dill

Butter

Chopped fresh watercress and parsley, for serving

Mix the oats, salmon, egg, onion, and dill by hand in a bowl.

Form the mixture into four flat patties, about the size of average burgers or less. (If the mixture won't come together into patties, add more oats.)

Melt the butter in a large pan over medium-high heat. Add the patties and fry until crispy on the bottom. Flip the patties and fry until they are crispy on the other side, too (about 6 to 7 minutes per side).

Serve with fresh watercress and parsley as a garnish.

——————————— ❋ ———————————

Learn the Runes of the Younger Futhark

The word *rune* comes from the Old Norse word *rún* (secret). You can learn the Viking alphabet of runes, known as the Younger Futhark, and use it to write secret magical messages! Write your phrase from left to right, using one or two dots to separate the words.

See the table on the next page for some of the runes that Fadir and Ulf might have carved into their Yule log.

THE YOUNGER FUTHARK

Shape	Sound	Name	Meaning
ᚡ	f	fé	wealth, cattle
ᚢ	u/o/v	úr	physical power on the physical plane
ᚦ	th/dh	thurs	giant, supernatural being on Earth
ᚬ	a	as/oss	one of the Gods
ᚱ	r	reið	travel, ride, wrath
ᚴ	k/g/ng	kaun	ulcer
ᚼ	h	hagall	hailstone
ᚾ	n	nauðr	need, lack of something
ᛁ	i/e	ísa/íss	ice
ᛅ	a	ár	fruitful year
ᛋ	s	sól	Sun, outer warmth coming to you
ᛏ	t/d/nt/nd	týr	courage, honor (taken from the name of the God Týr)
ᛒ	b/p/mb	björk/ bjarkan/ bjarken	birch, growth (birch is a healing plant noted for its rapid growth)
ᛘ	m	maðr	man, human
ᛚ	l	lögr	water, changeability
ᛦ	R	yr	yew tree, flexibility

Many thanks to Dr. Jane Sibley for the kennings (poetic meanings) in the list.

❋

Write Secret Rune Messages
with Invisible Ink

You can practice being a wise magician by using invisible ink. That way, your spells and intentions will be visible only to those who are worthy to see them.

- Put the juice of half a lemon and a few drops of water into a bowl or a cup and mix them carefully with a spoon.
- Strain the liquid into another cup.
- Dip a very clean fountain pen, a soft brush, or a quill (a feather with a sharpened end) into the lemon and water, and use it to write a message on a piece of plain white paper.
- Allow the message to air-dry.
- When you want someone else to read the message, tell them to hold the paper over a lightbulb. The lemon juice will turn brown when heated.

You can also do this with milk, onion juice, or white vinegar. Honey, yellow or red vinegar, orange juice, and wine work the same way but might be harder to hide because they have color. Try using them on paper with a little color to it.

3

LA BEFANA,
THE CHRISTMAS WITCH

An Italian Tale for the New Year
(January 1)

In Italian tradition, La Befana is the Christmas witch who brings gifts
to good children—and coal to the bad ones, much like Santa Claus—

on the night before the Christian festival of Epiphany on January 6. But La Befana has much deeper roots. She is said to be a modern version of the ancient Roman Goddess Strenua, whose festival honored the New Year and took place on January 1. Strenua is, of course, much older than Christianity.

※

It was the Winter Solstice—the darkest Moon on the darkest night at the darkest time of the year—and La Befana was still asleep in her high mountain refuge. She stirred, rolling over to make herself more comfortable on her large feather bed, and as she moved, a few white feathers billowed out from her pillows. They sailed out the window, turning into large, lazy snowflakes that rode the mountain winds and slowly drifted down onto the village below.

The next time she turned over, day was dawning and the very first fingers of the new year's sunlight illuminated the crags of her mountain home. La Befana was dreaming, remembering the days long ago when she was still revered as a Goddess.

In ancient Rome she had been known as Strenua, the Goddess who made the people active and strong. She was the bringer of good health, purification, strength, and gifts and even had her own temple at the head of the Via Sacra, Rome's main road.

Fragrant, sacred bay laurel trees grew within her temple precinct. On her feast day, January 1, people would exchange bunches of laurel bound with red thread, with each twig bearing exactly seven leaves. They also gave each other gifts of figs, dates, honey, and coins to carry sweetness into the new year. Carrying twigs from her sacred grove, celebrants marched in a grand procession from her shrine into the city to bless and purify the inhabitants.

But as time moved on, a new religion appeared, and Strenua was demoted. Now the people knew her only as a Faery or a witch, and they warned their children not to look for her too carefully. They said that like all Faeries, she preferred to stay invisible, and if anyone did happen to see her, she might thump them on the head with her broomstick!

One day, soon after the Winter Solstice, La Befana finally opened her eyes. A ray of sunlight had pierced the shadows on the mountain and prodded her awake. She yawned and stretched and then slowly rolled out of bed. She knew it was time to perform her divine duties, just as she had for thousands of years—bringing joy, strength, and purification to every home— and she began to assemble gifts to deliver on the eve of her special day.

The very first home she visited was always the house where three children, Nicolo, Matteo, and Lucia, now lived, because (even though they didn't realize it) their little stone hut was perched right on the side of her mountain. The children had been trying very hard to be good because they knew La Befana would soon be on her way. The last thing they wanted was a piece of coal or an onion or a bulb of garlic in their stocking! That had happened to their cousin Paolo the year before because he kept forgetting to feed the dog and had even cut off the tip of his sister's pigtail while she was sleeping (what a mean thing to do!).

Good children always got oranges and chocolates and nice new clothes, so this year Paolo was trying very hard to behave, too.

On this, the day before La Befana's arrival, their mother was busy baking a traditional La Befana cake, washing fruits, and soaking sweet chestnuts to put into dishes for the feast that night. Their father and uncles gathered wood into a great pile to make a bonfire for the celebration. They knew that La Befana's magic is especially associated with the hearth and with fire. The fire would carry their thoughts and wishes, and anything else put into it, skyward. As a winter spirit, La Befana would bless the fire and travel upward through the flames, taking the old year with her, renewing it and transforming it into a new year below. And that evening, Nonna, the children's grandmother, went to the well at the edge of town. She knew that water gathered on that night had magical properties and would protect the house and family from harm all year.

For the family, La Befana was a Faery, a witch, a wise woman, and a great magician, all rolled into one. She traveled on a magical *scopazzo,* a broom made with an ash-wood handle and birch twigs, which kept her in close contact with the trees and other nature spirits of the wild.

When La Befana was around, it was a good time to do divinations. For example, a sprig of sedum (stonecrop) could be left on the windowsill overnight. If it was perky and fresh the next day, it meant a new year of wealth and happiness. If it was wilted and limp in the morning, that meant your luck was running out.

Nonna did her own divination with flour. While making bread, she scooped out a small pile of flour to make a well in the center of the batter before adding the water and eggs. She could see images in the floury well when she poured in the liquid.

It was also a fine time to tell stories around the fire, such as how La Befana as a wise woman taught the people to be civilized—especially when she enforced the rules of good behavior in children!

A little La Befana doll hung on the family's Yule tree. She was dressed in a black dress and a black shawl so the soot she collected on her way down the chimney wouldn't show. La Befana was also known to ride a magical donkey, so a little donkey ornament hung beside her.

Nonna placed a plate of food and a glass of wine by the hearth as an offering to refresh La Befana when she came down the chimney. The offering always included a sprig of spearmint, bread, and cheese. La Befana would not actually eat the food, but she would absorb its essence, strengthening her for the nightlong journey. It made her very happy to receive these refreshments, because it reminded her of the gifts people used to bring to her in her ancient temple.

Nonna placed a new broom near the hearth in hopes that La Befana would bless it and sweep the floor before she left, clearing away the old year and bringing in the new.

Late that night, as the children slept and the grown-ups sipped *grappa* by the fire outside, La Befana did come. Invisible to everyone (except the family cat, who could see all the Faeries and spirits that entered the home), she blew on the new broom to bless it so it would purify the house all year. Then she touched and blessed each gift and piece of candy put out for the children to ensure their health, happiness, and protection.

And that year, even Paolo got the gifts he wanted!

🍃 BAY LAUREL TEA 🍃

Bay laurel is sacred to Strenua, and it's also a potent medicinal herb that can relieve digestive upset, a cold, a headache, or sleeplessness. You can make this tea and drink a cup of it to honor Strenua on her special day, drink the tea just for enjoyment as you wish, or you can take it by the quarter cup four times a day for one to two days (but no longer) to alleviate a cold, headache, insomnia, or tummy ache.

> 4 or 5 dried bay laurel leaves
> 1 cinnamon stick or 1 teaspoon ground cinnamon
> Milk (cow, soy, almond, cashew, coconut, rice, oat, hemp, or
>   flax), to taste
> Honey, to taste

Combine the bay laurel and cinnamon in a pot with 4 cups water. Bring to a boil, then reduce the heat and let simmer, covered, for 20 minutes. Strain out the herbs. Add milk and honey as desired (and thin the tea with more water if it's too strong).

Caution: Anyone who is pregnant or breastfeeding should avoid using bay laurel in medicinal dosages. Diabetics should monitor their blood sugar carefully when using this herb. And if you are taking any medications (including over-the-counter ones), check for possible contraindications or interactions before beginning to use any herb medicinally.

·················· **A Bit of Lore about Bay Laurel** ················

Bay laurel (*Laurus nobilis*) is sacred to the Goddess Strenua and, by association, La Befana. But it has a long history of use in medicine, magic, and spirituality. It was used by priestesses of the temple of Apollo—the God of music, poetry, sunlight, prophecy, and medicine—at Delphi in Greece. In those days, bay laurel was thought of as a magical plant that could enhance prophetic powers and protect a person from both diseases and sorcery. The ancient Greeks and Romans crowned victorious athletes with wreaths of bay laurel as a sign of their divine favor.

In the Middle Ages, bay laurel was taken as a medicine for stomach issues and for colic and kidney diseases.

Modern herbalists use it to treat digestive problems, flu, bronchitis, anxiety, sleeplessness, and migraine. It is used externally to poultice bruises and sprains and as a hair wash for dandruff.

. . . .

🌿 LA BEFANA CAKE 🌿

For this cake it is important to use organic lemons and oranges because conventionally grown fruits often carry a large amount of pesticide on their peels.

> 1½ tablespoons chopped candied orange peel (see next page)
> 1½ tablespoons minced candied ginger
> 2 tablespoons finely chopped dried apricots or cranberries
> 2 tablespoons raisins or currants
> ¼ cup grappa or other brandy
> 3½ cups milk (cow, soy, almond, cashew, coconut, rice, oat, hemp, or flax)
> 1 teaspoon sea salt
> 1¼ cups cornmeal
> ¾ cup almond flour or wheat cake flour
> ⅓ cup butter, softened
> ¾ cup diced fresh apple
> ¾ cup brown sugar or 1 cup raw, local honey, plus a little brown sugar to sprinkle on top
> 1½ teaspoons anise seeds
> 1½ teaspoons fennel seeds
> 2 teaspoons grated lemon or orange zest
> Slivered almonds, candied fruit, fresh mint, pine tips, and any other decorations you might desire

Soften the orange peel, ginger, apricots, and raisins by soaking them in the brandy for about 1 hour.

Preheat the oven to 350°F. Lightly butter an 8- to 9-inch round springform cake pan.

Pour the milk into a large pot. Bring to a boil, then lower the heat immediately and add the salt. Stir in the cornmeal and almond flour, whisking to remove any lumps.

Cook over low heat, stirring continuously, for about 11 minutes (add more milk if the mixture gets too thick).

Remove from the heat and drop in the butter (in small chunks), apple, brown sugar, anise seed, fennel seed, lemon or orange zest, and soaked fruit.

Mix everything together and pour into the prepared cake pan.

Level the surface of the batter and sprinkle with a bit of brown sugar.

Bake for 50 to 55 minutes, until the top is golden brown (bake for 7 to 10 minutes longer if you used honey in the batter).

Allow to cool and set overnight.

The cake will be round and yellow like the returning Sun. Decorate it as you wish; I like to use slivered almonds, rounds of candied orange or lemon slices, and a few sprigs of fresh mint or pine tips.

Make Your Own Candied Orange Peel

Cut the top and bottom off two large oranges, then, with a peeler or sharp knife, cut the peel into ¼-inch-thick strips, boil the strips in plain water for 15 minutes, then rinse well. Next bring 3 cups of water and 3 cups of sugar to a boil, add in the strips of peel, bring to a boil again, and then simmer for about 45 minutes until the strips are very soft. Drain the cooked peels, then roll them in 1 cup raw sugar until they are completely coated. Set them on a paper towel and let them dry overnight or until they harden. You can make these ahead of time, wrap them in a paper towel and freeze them in an airtight container for up to two months.

_____

This recipe is adapted from Danielle Prohom Olson, "La Befana Cake: Honouring the Old Witch of Winter," Gather Victoria (website), December 18, 2018.

——————————————— ❋ ———————————————

Make Your Own Besom—A Magical Broom

La Befana travels the world on her broom, and you can honor her by making one. Leave it out on the night of January 5 for La Befana to bless. You can use it to ritually sweep bad vibes and energies out of the house all year or to purify a ceremonial area.

Traditionally a besom is made with an ash-wood handle and birch twigs, but you can use any of the trees listed on page 16. Just pay attention to the qualities of the tree you pick! You can even make a besom with feathers, thick grasses, or other long, pliable materials. (If you do use grasses or dry natural fibers, first soak them in water overnight to make them flexible.)

This kind of broom is more of a prop or ritual object than a really sturdy broom for cleaning the house, so don't worry about how professional it looks.

- Gather your twigs, trim them so they are the same length, and lay them on the ground in as tight a bundle as you can manage. The thicker ends of the twigs should be at the top and the thinner ends at the bottom.
- Trim the top of the bundle so the thick ends are neatly cut and even. Use garden shears or, if your branches are very thin, scissors.
- Leave the bottom ends loose, flowing, and slightly flared out.
- Tie the top of the bundle of twigs with wire or natural twine, going around the bundle several times and weaving in and out a few times. Keep going until the bundle is very tight and secure.
- Get a fairly straight, thick branch for your handle. Peel off the bark, or not, as you please. (A crooked handle works, too.)
- Find the middle of your twig bundle and push the handle down into it.

- Turn the broom upside down and, holding the bundle tightly, bash it into the ground a few times to more securely insert the handle.
- Tie more wire or string around the top of the twig bundle if needed, or insert a few nails through the twigs and into the handle to fasten everything securely.

Example of a simple besom

Now that you have a besom, you can ritually clean the house. "Sweep" every room out as you sing or chant, starting with the corners, then sweeping to the middle of the room and finally out the door. Have a person follow you with a bowl of saltwater, sprinkling it around each room you have swept. A third person should follow with a white candle and hold it up to all the dark places in each room (corners, closets, and so on).

Go through every room of the house this way, singing or chanting and sweeping out any disquiet energies. End by sweeping all the energies out the back door.

Do not use the broom for everyday cleaning. Instead, store it somewhere safe and special, bristle side up, or hang it on a wall. If you like, you can personalize your besom with stones, feathers, crystals, and other symbols that are meaningful to you.

When you're ready to travel, sit with your besom or lie down with it by your side and visualize yourself flying through the air to speak with the spirits and the Faeries or even La Befana herself!

4

WAITING FOR BRIGHID

An Irish Tale for Imbolg
(February 1–2)

Gods, Goddesses, Spirits, and Magical Beings:

Brighid (*breej*)—a Goddess of healing, poetry, smithcraft, childbirth, motherhood, and inspiration. A Fire Goddess of the forge, the fire in the belly (sustenance and health), and the fire in the head (poetic inspiration). Her name means "exalted one."

Irish and Celtic Words to Know:

brat Brighde (*BRAHT BREE-juh*)—Brighid's mantle, a cloth ribbon, cloak, band, or scarf that is put out for Brighid to bless on Imbolg night so that it can be used in healing work all year.

Brídeóg (*BREED-hogue*)—a Brighid doll, also called a Biddy, made from rushes, reeds, or straw and dressed in white cloth, shells, or flowers. She is laid in a bed by the fire, and a magic wand is placed beside her, symbolic of the Goddess's ability to transform the weather.

Rag Tree—a tree with small strips of cloth hung on it, endowed with healing power. The rags would be hung on a tree over a sacred well as a type of prayer flag or tied to an ailing person or animal to help them heal.

daidí (*DAH-dee*)—father.

> **Imbolg (*IH-molg*)**—a Celtic festival held on February 1–2
> celebrating the lactation of ewes, who give birth at about
> this time, and the Goddess Brighid. A medieval term for the
> festival is Oimelc, "ewe's milk."
>
> **mamaí (*MAH-mee*)**—mother

. . . .

This tale is about the festival of Imbolg, which literally means "in the belly." It is also sometimes called Oimelc, which means "ewe's milk." Ewes are female sheep, and this is essentially a milk festival in celebration of the lactation of the ewes.

In modern times we can easily go to the supermarket, even in the middle of winter, and pick up a gallon of milk. In ancient times many people had only sheep's milk. The sheep were ready to mate in the fall, gestated (grew babies in their bellies) for about five months, and didn't give milk again until three days or so before giving birth, around February 1. The reappearance of the milk coincided with the noticeable strengthening of the sunlight and everyone was very excited when the milk reappeared, especially the children.

The Goddess of this festival is Brighid, a Fire Goddess and the great Triple Goddess of Healing, Smithcraft, and Poetry, as well as of childbirth and motherhood.

✳

The birds noticed it first. The sunlight had grown and grown until the sky was as bright and clear and blue as a robin's egg. Wrens, thrushes, and finches darted in and out of the branches of the old sycamore tree, excited to be sharing the news. The light had returned!

Little yellow-orange buds were already swelling at the tips of the branches, and the old tree was bursting with sap. Some of the sugary liquid dripped and oozed its way out of cracks in the bark. A little red squirrel ran up and down the tree taking licks of sweetness, a treasure she could get only once a year.

The ground was veiled with a silvery blanket of snow, and the little pond at the end of the lane was still girdled with ice. Every afternoon, when Daidí took a break from his work in the barn, Áine* would meet him at the door and they would walk hand in hand down the stony path that led out of the farmyard.

"We need to check the fields every day now," Daidí said.

"Why?" Áine asked.

"Because it's almost time!" Daidí replied.

"Time for what?"

"You'll see!" said Daidí with a wink.

Each day when they got past the gate and the sheep barn and the tool shed, Daidí would bend and probe the frozen ground with his fingers.

"Why do you do that?" asked Áine.

"Because I am waiting for Brighid to come," Daidí replied.

"Who is she?" asked Áine, who was only five but thought she had already met all the relatives and everyone who lived in the village.

Daidí looked up at the noonday sky, gazing for a few seconds at the Sun.

"She is the great Fire Goddess of spring," he said. "Wherever she walks the land, the frost disappears. And when she puts her finger into a pond or a lake, the ice melts. *That's* how we know she has been here."

Áine looked around and noticed frozen puddles still dotting little hollows in the fields. "I guess she hasn't been here yet!" she exclaimed.

The next day, when Áine went to the barn Daidí said, "Let's go and inspect the sheep."

"Why?" asked Áine.

"Because they will tell us if Brighid has been here!"

"They will?" Áine asked, bewildered. "I didn't know that sheep can talk!"

"They won't use *words*," said Daidí, "but if their udders are full of milk

---

*Áine's name is pronounced *AWN-ye.*

and their bellies are full of babies, we will know that the time of Brighid is here."

And so, they went into the barn to inspect the sheep and feel their bellies.

"It's almost time!" exclaimed Daidí.

The next afternoon they went down the stony path again. This time Daidí led Áine farther up the hill and into the forest.

"Where are we going now?" asked Áine.

"You'll see!" said Daidí, and they climbed and climbed until they reached a sunny patch between some large rocks where the Sun-warmed stones had made the ground soft and brown. Daidí was looking around for something.

"What are you searching for?" asked Áine.

"You'll see!" said Daidí.

Something long and brown and twisty darted past their feet. It was a snake!

Áine let out a little scream.

"That's just what I was looking for!" Daidí exclaimed. "You see, when it's warm enough for a snake or a badger to come out of her underground home, that means Brighid is coming!"

The next day they went out to the fields, and Daidí tested the earth with his fingers again. This time the soil was peaty and soft to the touch.

"The land is almost ready for plowing!" Daidí said with a smile. "Do you see those blooming bushes covered in white flowers at the edge of the field? Those are blackthorns. Once they bloom, that means Brighid is near!"

When they got back to the barn, Áine saw the sheep's swollen udders.

"The sheep are ready to give milk!" she exclaimed.

There had been no milk to drink for many months, and Áine wanted some *sooo* badly. She was very tired of eating her porridge with no milk.

"Mamaí still has to do her work in the barn by candlelight, but soon it will be light enough to work without a taper," Daidí said. "That's another sign that Brighid is coming! Yes, Brighid is coming very soon," he added. "In fact, she will be here this very eve!"

They walked back to the house, and Mamaí was waiting there with fresh green rushes she had cut that very afternoon. "After supper we will make our Brighid crosses!" she said. "And I will put out our *brat Brighde* for her to bless this night. That's the white cloth I always put around your shoulders when you are feeling sick or have a cold. You can leave out strips of old, worn cloth for her blessing, too. We can tie those around the necks of the animals when they get sick."

Áine, Mamaí, and Daidí worked long into the night making equal-armed rush crosses to represent the Sun so they could hang them in the windows and hide them in the roof thatch for luck.

"We need to leave a gift for Brighid to thank her for all her help," said Mamaí.

"What should we give her?" Áine asked.

"We will make new butter, and we'll leave out a nice dish of porridge with a big pat of butter on top that is as golden as the sunlight," said Mamaí. "I will also make her oaten bread and leave some by the door. And I will put out a thick candle whose light will guide her to our house and barn!

"We shall also make a Brídeóg," said Mamaí, "a little doll made of straw to represent Brighid and the magic wand that she uses to change the weather, and we'll make a bed to lay her in near the hearth. She can rest there if she needs to, and we will inspect the ashes in the morning to see if she has left her footprint."

And so, they did all those things. When Áine woke the next day, she ran straight to the hearth to see if Brighid had left a footprint. And she had!

When they all went outside to collect the brat Brighde, the little strips of cloth, and the crosses that had been left out to be blessed, they were amazed. The land had completely transformed!

Gone was the icing of snow on the fields, and gone were the frosty puddles. The air was soft and the birds were singing. In the barn, the sheep had started giving birth, and their udders were full of rich, warm milk.

"Now we can have milk on our porridge again!" exclaimed Áine.

"Now I can start to plow!" said Dadaí.

"And now I can do my milking without a candle!" said Mamaí.

And they were very happy.

☙ IRISH OATMEAL SODA BREAD ☙

Coming as it does at the very time when the dairy animals begin to give milk, the traditional Imbolg feast features dairy products such as new butter, cheese, and yogurt. Serve this bread warm and slathered with soft cheese or butter, in honor of the Imbolg festival, and be sure to leave a thick slice on the doorstep as a gift to Brighid on Imbolg Eve.

2 cups old-fashioned rolled oats

2¼ cups all-purpose flour, plus more for dusting your work
    surface

2 teaspoons baking soda

1 teaspoon sugar or ½ teaspoon raw, local honey

1 teaspoon sea salt

1½ cups buttermilk

1 egg, lightly beaten

Butter, for greasing the pan

Preheat the oven to 450°F.

Place the oats in a food processor and pulse until they are finely ground.

Whisk together the dry ingredients: the finely ground oats, flour, baking soda, sugar, and salt.

In a separate bowl, stir the buttermilk and egg together until well blended.

Make a well in the middle of the flour mixture, and pour the buttermilk and egg mixture into it. Gently fold the surrounding flour over the liquid with a wooden spoon, but do not overmix! The dough should look very shaggy and be on the moist side. If it is too wet to handle, add a little more flour. If too dry, add a little more buttermilk.

Lightly dust a work surface with flour and place the dough on it. Knead the dough one or two times only and then form it into a mound.

Grease a large cast-iron frying pan with a little butter and place the dough in the center. (If you don't have a cast-iron frying pan, just put the dough on a greased baking sheet.)

Use a sharp knife to score the center of the dough in the shape of a Brighid's cross (see page 55), making 1½-inch-deep cuts.

Bake in the oven for 15 minutes at 450°F, then lower the oven temperature to 400°F and bake for 25 minutes longer.

To test if the bread is done, take the pan out of the oven, turn the loaf over, and knock on the bottom. If it sounds hollow, it's done.

Let the bread rest in the pan for 10 minutes. Then remove it from the pan and let it cool on a wire rack for another 15 minutes or so.

The bread is best when eaten within hours of baking. Serve it with real butter and jam. If you're saving it for later, wrap it in a slightly damp, clean tea towel.

This recipe is adapted from Elise Bauer, "Oatmeal Soda Bread," Simply Recipes (website), February 11, 2021.

🍂 HOMEMADE BUTTER 🌿

Fresh butter is a welcome addition to the Imbolg feasting table! Note that the heavy whipping cream is important. You cannot use low-fat or light cream; it will not make butter.

> 1 pint heavy whipping cream
> A jar with a tight-fitting lid
> A bowl of ice water
> Sea salt, optional

Pour the cream into the jar, cap it, and shake vigorously.

Keep shaking for at least fifteen minutes. Eventually butter will form!

Once the butter has solidified, pour off the liquid. That's buttermilk, and you can use it for baking or drink it.

Scoop the butter into a bowl. Rinse the butter by pouring the ice water over it. Using a small spatula or a spoon, press the butter into the ice water, squeezing out any remaining buttermilk.

Pour off the water and repeat. Keep rinsing and squishing the butter with the ice water until the water remains clear after pressing.

Add some sea salt, if you like, and work it through the butter.

Pack the butter into a container, cover it, and store it in the refrigerator.

Note: You can make herbed butter by folding in minced chives, garlic, or other herbs. You can make honey butter by folding in raw honey.

***

Make a Brighid's Cross for Imbolg

Brighid's cross is an ancient Sun symbol. It takes the strength and light of the Sun to grow the grains and grasses. By hanging Brighid's cross on your wall, placing it in a window, hiding it in the eaves, or setting it over the doorway, you are bringing the strength and luck of the harvest into your home.

- Gather fresh rushes if they grow in your area, or soak dried straw or reeds overnight in the bathtub. You will need sixteen pieces to work with.
- Take the shortest straw and hold it upright.
- Fold a second straw in half.
- Wrap the second straw around the middle of the first straw so that the opening faces right.
- Pull it tight.
- Rotate the straws counterclockwise so the second (bent) straw points straight up.
- Fold and wrap a third straw around the second straw so the opening points to the right.
- Pull it tight.

Sample of a finished Brighid's cross.
Photo by Culnacreann.

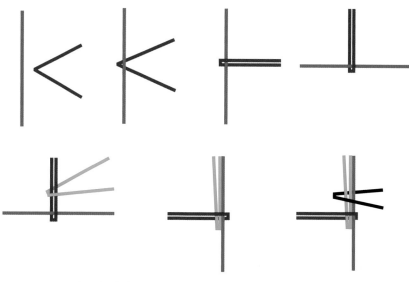

Visual of the steps for making Brighid's cross

- Rotate the straws counterclockwise again, keeping hold of the center.
- Fold and wrap a fourth straw around the third straw so it opens to the right.
- Pull it tight.
- Rotate the straws counterclockwise again, keeping hold of the center.
- Fold and wrap a fifth straw around the fourth straw so it opens to the right.
- Pull it tight.
- Keep folding, wrapping, pulling tight, and rotating the straws until you have used all of them.
- Tie off the ends of the four arms of the cross with twine, rope, or ribbons. Trim the ends with scissors so they are even.

--- ❇ ---

Make a Straw Brídeog (Brighid Doll)

You can make a Brighid doll out of wheat, straw, dried grasses, corn husks, reeds, and a variety of similar materials. Take a walk in nature and see what you can find! I do this every year in the summer and save the grasses and wheat I find to use the next spring. If you can't do that, then go to a craft store and purchase some bunches of dried wheat.

- The night before you make your doll, lay the straw or grasses in a bathtub or laundry tub and cover them with cold water. Let them soak until you are ready to work.
- Pat the straw dry with a towel and then lay the pieces out on a table so they are all facing the same way.
- Divide the straw into two piles: one larger, thicker pile for the body of the doll, and a smaller pile for the arms.
- Take the larger, thicker bunch and tie it off just above the seed

These are photos of a Brighid doll I made for
Imbolg. Notice the crystal tied to the center
of the doll. The purple plaid is my brat Brighde,
which I use for healing all the next year. The photo
shows a "Brighid's girdle," which is a rope with three Brighid crosses hung on
it; you step through the girdle for luck. The basket holds little strips of cloth
to use for healing work during the coming year. The candle is left burning
all night to guide Brighid to my door, and a bowl of oatmeal with cream and
honey is left out in a crystal bowl as an offering. You can also leave out your
yearly store of candles for her to bless! Photos by Kate Devlin.

heads or grains to make a skirt. As you tie the knot, make a wish and then breathe onto the knot.

⚹ Bend the top of the bunch over to make a head and tie that down. Again, as you tie the knot, make a wish and then breathe onto the knot. Leave any seed heads in place to make hair.

⚹ Now gather together the smaller pile and tie it at each end to make arms. Make a wish and breathe onto the knots as you tie them.

⚹ Push the arms through the top of the doll's body and then tie them to the body with more string. Make a wish and breathe onto the knots as you tie them.

⚹ Dress the doll in white cloth. If you like, you can affix crystals, shells, flowers, and other decorations to it.

⚹ Put the doll outside overnight on Imbolg Eve (February 1) for Brighid to bless, or make a little bed by a fireplace and lay the doll in it. If you set it by the fireplace, be sure to examine the ashes the next morning to see if Brighid has been there. If so, she will leave her footprint!

After Imbolg, you can keep the doll on your altar, if you have one. Some people hang the doll on the wall. Others bury it in the ground in spring because the grain might sprout. In ancient Scotland, one corner of a farm field, called the Goodman's croft (*Goodman* is another word for "Faery"), was always left wild. That would be a good place to bury a Brighid doll. Another place would be in a field about to be planted or on top of a hill.

A Poem for Imbolg

Goddess of Fire in times of old,
Brighid walks the land.

Born on a hill in a shaft of light,
Brighid walks the land.

Visiting doors on the eve of her feast,
Brighid walks the land.

Blessing the rags and the brat in the entrance,
Brighid walks the land.

Sharing the oatmeal left out for her pleasure,
Brighid walks the land.

Blessing the candles for use all the year,
Brighid walks the land.

Ice melts where she walks as the snow fades away,
Brighid walks the land.

Bulbs burst open and snowdrops appear,
Brighid walks the land.

Now on the hillsides the green is returning,
Brighid walks the land.

The fires of life are kindling and burning,
Brighid walks the land!

5

EOSTRE, THE GODDESS OF SPRING, HARES, AND EGGS

An Anglo-Saxon/Germanic Tale for the Spring Equinox (March 19/20/21)

····················· **Key Figures and Terms** ·················
Gods, Goddesses, Spirits, and Magical Beings:
    Eostre (*YOW-str*)—a Goddess of the spring.
Anglo-Saxon/Germanic Words to Know:
    oma (*OH-mah*)—grandmother.
··

Have you ever wondered why we have Easter eggs and bunnies? Rabbits don't lay eggs, and yet we associate both bunnies and colorful eggs with the spring festival of rebirth and goodies in baskets. This tale will explain it all and tell you about the Goddess Eostre, for whom Easter is named.

✳

Henrik and Annemie* led a very unusual life. They lived with their *oma*, or grandmother, in a tiny thatched cottage deep in the forest. Oma didn't care if they did their lessons or combed their hair or even if they finished their beans at dinner. She always said there were more important things in

---

*Henrik's name is pronounced *HEHN-rihk*. Annemie's is *ANN-eh-me*.

61

life, like knowing where the otters hid their slide into the river, and where the wild swans nested, and which herbs were good for a wound or a cough.

Since they didn't have a calendar in the house, Oma taught Henrik and Annemie to read the signs of nature so that they would know which month of the year they were in.

"Do you know where the word *month* comes from?" Oma asked early one morning as they were setting out with woven wicker baskets to pick spring greens for their supper.

"Hmmmm . . . ," said Henrik, who liked to think long and deeply about things and thought of himself as a philosopher of the mysteries of life.

"No clue," said Annemie, who liked to read books by candlelight.

"It comes from the word *Moonth,*" said Oma.

"*Moonth* isn't a word!" said Annemie, who was very sure she had never seen *Moonth* in a book.

"Well, it may not be a word in your books, but it certainly is the way Mother Nature organizes her calendar," said Oma. "Let's go out tonight and see what happens under the March full Moon. You might learn something!"

Oma didn't care if they went to bed on time, either.

After a supper of soup made with the fresh greens they had just picked and slices of warm, grainy bread topped with goat's cheese and wild violet flowers (yes, you can eat those!), they put on their warmest cloaks, hats, and mittens—the spring air was still chilly at night. Annemie lit a small lantern that contained a single beeswax candle, and Oma filled a thermos with hot herbal tea. Then Henrik unbolted the oaken front door to their cottage and out the door they trooped, into the misty night.

The path through the forest stretched before them, easily visible in the bright moonlight. Oma had taught them to be very quiet in the dark woods and to talk in whispers, and only when it was absolutely necessary. They were so quiet that they could hear owls conversing overhead while mice rustled in the leaves at their feet. A deer crossed the path right in front of them and didn't even notice they were there!

Soon they came to a large open heath where the spring grasses and heather were already thick and long. Moonlight glistened on the damp meadow. "We can sit down here," Oma whispered.

They hunkered down and were very still. Any person or animal walking by would have thought they were just three large rocks in the middle of the field. They waited for a while, enjoying the stars and the soft spring breeze.

Suddenly there was a flurry of movement at the far end of the field. And it—whatever it was—was coming closer!

"What could that be?" wondered Henrik in a loud whisper. He was scared he might have to defend his grandmother and sister from a bear or a wolf. Annemie slid closer to Oma so they would look like a bigger lump to whatever was coming toward them.

Then the grass seemed to part and the *thing*—whatever it was—was right in front of them. It was a crazy moving tangle of hares! Suddenly hares were everywhere, jumping and chasing and boxing each other. The ones that weren't doing that were just sitting and gazing, looking up at the full Moon.

"See how the hares are dancing?" said Oma. "Some say that witches shape-shift into hares under the full Moon during the Spring Equinox."

"That's when day and night are equal in length and the Sun rises exactly in the east and sets exactly in the west," added Henrik, in a professorial tone of voice.

"I know *that*," said Annemie, who had already read about it in a book.

"Look closely at the hares and see if you can find one that is white and larger than the rest," Oma whispered.

Henrik and Annemie squinted and stared until finally they did see one that seemed to stand out.

"I think I see it!" whispered Annemie.

"Who is that?" whispered Henrik. "Is it the king of the hares?"

"Well," said Oma, "this time of year is sacred to a particular Goddess. Her name is Eostre, and she has a large white hare that goes with her wherever she travels. You might be seeing that hare now! Eostre herself takes the form of a hare at every full Moon. All hares are sacred to her. They are her messengers."

"Messengers?" squeaked Henrik. "Who do they take messages to?"

"When hares burrow underground, they commune with the spirits, and then they bring messages from the Faeries and the ancestors back up to the world of the living," explained Oma. "But Eostre has one extra-special white hare that lays colored eggs just for children every year at exactly this time of year!"

"Is that how we get them in our baskets?" asked Annemie.

"Yes! That is why we always put out a basket at this time of the year," said Oma. "And have you noticed that the days are getting longer and longer now?"

"Oh yes," said Henrik, who was very glad he could stay out just a little later each day to study bugs and frogs and other interesting creatures.

"That's because Eostre is followed by a long procession of hares carrying torches, and each morning when she rises at dawn, they follow her," Oma told them. "As they approach, the light grows stronger and stronger, and the strengthening light tells the birds that it's time to lay their eggs. So, we celebrate with colored eggs. Easter is named for Eostre, and that's why we have Easter bunnies and Easter eggs!"

As they watched, the hares leaped higher and higher, as if they were trying to touch the Moon. Oma, Henrik, and Annemie sipped their warm tea, enjoying the spectacle. When they started to feel the cold and damp, Oma said it was time to go home. And so they went.

The next morning, when Henrik and Annemie got up, their baskets were filled with beautiful colored eggs and lots of sweets like cookies, candy, and dried fruits.

"I hope you will never forget how magical these eggs are, brought to you by Eostre's special bunny," said Oma. "The Goddess Eostre always carries with her a basket of newly laid eggs. They hold the promise of new beginnings and the yearly resurrection of nature after the long sleep of winter. Every time you see an egg, know that it is blessed by Eostre, and give thanks."

And do you know, that is just what they did.

❦ HOT CROSS BUNS ❧

Did you know that in ancient times the equal-armed cross was a symbol of the Sun? That's why these crosses are placed on freshly baked buns—to celebrate the strengthening sunlight and warmth of spring!

For the buns:

¼ cup apple juice, black tea, or water

½ cup mixed dried fruits, such as diced apricots, yellow raisins, cranberries, or even a pinch of grated orange zest or minced candied citrus peel

½ cup raisins or dried black currants

1¼ cups milk (cow, soy, almond, cashew, coconut, rice, oat, hemp, or flax)

2 large eggs, plus one extra yolk (save the egg white for the glaze)

6 tablespoons butter, softened

4½ cups all-purpose flour (gluten-free flour works as well as wheat flour)

¼ cup packed light brown sugar

1 tablespoon baking powder

2 teaspoons instant yeast

1¾ teaspoons sea salt

1 teaspoon ground cinnamon

¼ teaspoon ground cloves or allspice

¼ teaspoon ground nutmeg

For the glaze:

1 egg white

1 tablespoon milk (cow, soy, almond, cashew, coconut, rice, oat, hemp, or flax)

For the icing:

1 cup, plus 2 tablespoons confectioners' sugar

½ teaspoon pure vanilla extract

> 1 teaspoon orange juice* or grated orange zest, optional
>
> A pinch of sea salt
>
> 4 teaspoons milk (cow, soy, almond, cashew, coconut, rice, oat, hemp, or flax)
>
> _____
>
> *If you use orange juice in the icing, add a bit more confectioners' sugar to keep the icing thick and pipeable.

Grease a 10-inch square pan or a 9-inch x 13-inch pan.

Warm the apple juice in a pot, then add the mixed dried fruits and raisins. Let them soak while you mix up the rest of the ingredients.

Combine the milk, eggs, butter, flour, brown sugar, baking powder, yeast, salt, cinnamon, cloves, and nutmeg in a large bowl and mix well.

Grease your hands (so the dough doesn't stick). Knead the dough until it is soft and elastic.

Mix in the soaked fruit and any liquid still left in the pot.

Place the dough in a bowl, cover with a cloth, and let rise for 1 hour, until it becomes puffy.

Grease your hands again. Divide the dough into pieces about the size of billiard balls. You should have enough for twelve to fourteen of them.

Shape each piece into a round ball. Arrange the balls of dough in the greased pan. Let them rise for 1 hour, until they are puffy and touching each other.

Preheat the oven to 375°F.

Make the glaze by whisking together the egg white and tablespoon of milk. Brush it over the buns.

Bake for 20 minutes, until the buns are golden brown on top.

Carefully transfer the buns to a wire rack to cool.

Mix together the icing ingredients. When the buns are cool, pipe an equal-armed cross onto each bun. You can use a ziplock bag as a piping tool; just scoop the icing into the bag, snip off a corner, and squeeze the icing through the opening.

_____

This recipe is adapted from "Easy Hot Cross Buns," King Arthur Baking Company (website), accessed January 20, 2020.

❧ OMA'S SPRING GREENS SOUP ❧

After you pick the greens, soak them for twenty minutes in a quart or so of water with a few teaspoons of vinegar or sea salt added, and then rinse them; this will remove any bugs. When picking nettles, be careful—they can sting. Wear sturdy gloves (like rubber kitchen gloves) and use scissors to clip the nettle greens, and then rinse them under cold water for a minute. The sting will disappear almost immediately.

- 2 cups freshly gathered young nettle tops or baby nettles (less than 6 inches high)
- 1½ cups freshly gathered dandelion greens (pick the top half of the leaves)
- 8 cups water, divided
- 2 tablespoons virgin olive oil
- 1 large onion, chopped
- ½ cup wild ramps, green onions (scallions), or garlic scapes
- 2 turnips or 2–3 carrots, chopped (about 1 cup)
- 2 cups chopped winter squash, red or white potatoes, or sweet potatoes
- Miso, vegetable stock, or soy sauce, to taste, optional

Soak, rinse, and chop the nettles and dandelion greens. Simmer in 2 cups of the water (or as much water as you need to cover them) until they are very tender (about 15 minutes).

Warm the olive oil in a pan over medium heat. Add the onion and sauté until golden, about 5 minutes.

Add the ramps, turnips, and squash to the pan.

Add the remaining 6 cups water. Bring to a simmer, and let simmer for about 30 minutes, or until the vegetables are very tender.

Turn off the heat. Stir in the miso (or vegetable stock or soy sauce) to taste, right before serving.

This recipe is adapted from Winnie Abramson, "Spring Tonic Soup with Wild Greens," Healthy Green Kitchen (website), May 2, 2013.

❋

Use Herbs and Fruits to Dye Easter Eggs

Back in the days before you could run to the store to buy egg-dying kits full of chemicals, you would have used natural herbs and berries to dye Easter eggs. You can still do that today—and honor Eostre, the Goddess of spring, and her role in the natural cycles of the world.

- Hard-cook in water any eggs you want to dye (you can also cook the eggs in the prepared dyewater, which will make them even more colorful).
- Measure out a few cups of water—enough that you can soak all your hard-cooked eggs in the water. Bring the water to a boil, then pour it into a large bowl.
- Add 2 teaspoons of vinegar per cup of hot water. Let cool.
- When the water has cooled, add your eggs and let them soak for 5 minutes.

Easter eggs dyed naturally.
Photo by Cheryl.

➤ Remove the eggs and rinse them with cold water. (The vinegar rinse makes the surface of the egg porous so that it will more easily absorb the dyes.)

➤ Prepare your dyes (see the box below) and pour the colored waters into glass jars.

➤ Add the eggs to the jars. Let them soak for as long as you like. The longer you steep the eggs in the dye, the deeper the color will be.

Tips!

• Stir alum powder, a pickling spice you can find in grocery stores, into the dyes to deepen the color.

• Cooking the eggs in the dye rather than boiling them beforehand will also make the colors more intense.

• To make designs on an egg, use a wax candle to drip a pattern onto its shell before you place the egg in the dye bath. Simmer the egg in hot water to melt off the wax afterward. Or attach stickers to an egg before it goes into the dye bath, and remove the stickers after the egg comes out.

• To make speckled eggs, put a few drops of vegetable oil into the dye bath. The oil will prevent the dye from adhering in some spots and cause a speckled effect.

Make Natural Dyes for Easter Eggs

Simmer any of the following in water to make a natural dye. The longer the eggs steep in the colored liquid, the deeper their color will be.

For red, use crushed raspberries, beets, cherries, cranberries, or blackberries.

For pink, use beet juice and vinegar together—about 1 cup pickled beet juice and 1 tablespoon vinegar—or red grape juice, hibiscus flowers, strawberries, or red rose petals.

For gold/orange, use onion skins—yellow onion skins will dye the eggs a light tan-orange, red onion skins will yield a richer brown-gold color—or 1 cup turmeric powder with a tablespoon white vinegar added (soak a brown egg in turmeric for three hours or a white or brown egg in turmeric overnight). You can also use paprika or annatto seeds.

For yellow, use turmeric powder (soak a white egg in turmeric for three hours), citrus peels, or yellow onion skins.

For green, use carrot tops, green tea powder, spinach, or other greens, or red onion skins with a little vinegar (the reaction with the vinegar turns them green).

For dark blue, use sliced red cabbage just covered with water and simmered until tender.

For purple, use purple grape juice, whole red grapes, blackberries, or lavender flowers.

For brown, use coffee, black tea, walnut husks, or cumin seeds.

Spring Is Coming!

"Spring is coming!"
said the seed,
dreaming of being a weed.

"Spring is coming!"
said the root,
putting out a shoot.

"Spring is coming!"
said the crocus,
opening to the Sun.

"Spring is coming!"
said the pussy willows,
purring on their stems.

"Spring is coming!"
said the mouse,
cleaning out her house.

"Spring is coming!"
said the fish,
under the melting ice.

"Spring is coming!"
said the loon,
gliding on the lake.

"Spring is coming!"
said the mother fox,
deep within her den.

"Spring is coming!"
said the snake,
testing the air.

"Spring is coming!"
said the hedgehog,
rolling down the hill.

"Spring is coming!"
said the bear,
from deep within her lair.

"Spring is coming!"
said the hare,
dancing beneath the Moon.

"Spring is coming!"
said the robins,
feathering their nest.

"Spring is coming!"
said the sheep,
nursing her lamb.

"Spring is coming!"
said the rose,
putting out a bud.

"SPRING IS HERE!"
said Eostre,
the Goddess of spring.

"Yes, spring is here!"
said the hare,
with her big basket of eggs!

6

A MAGICAL BELTAINE JOURNEY

An Irish Tale for May Day
(May 1)

· · · · · · · · · · · · · · · · **Key Figures and Terms** · · · · · · · · · · · · · · · ·

Gods, Goddesses, Spirits, and Magical Beings:

> **Lunantisidhe (*loo-NAN-tih-shee*)**—a type or tribe of Faeries; the name means "Moon Faeries."
>
> **Sidhe (*shee*)**—the Faeries.

Irish Words to Know:

> **Beltaine (*BELL-tayn*)**—the Celtic May Day festival, when herds of animals (like cows and sheep) were ritually blessed by having them pass between two great fires on their way up to their summer pasture in the hills. The traditional Irish spelling is Bealtaine (*be-OWL-tin-eh*).
>
> **Druids (*DREW-ids*)**—ritual leaders, magicians, soothsayers, and experts in law, herbalism, philosophy, poetry, natural sciences, and other specialties of ancient Celtic society (and Druids still exist today!).
>
> **mamaí (*MAH-mee*)**—mother.
>
> **ogham (*OH-ahm*)**—an alphabet that was used primarily to write the early Irish language, from the fourth to the ninth centuries.
>
> **Tir na nÓg (*TEER nah nog*)**—literally, "land of youth," meaning the land of the Faeries.

> uilleann (*ILL-ee-un or ILL-un*)—literally, "of the elbow."
> Playing bagpipes requires you to push air through the
> pipes. To play Irish uilleann pipes, you hold the bellows (a
> bag of air) under your elbow and squeeze the bag to push
> out the air.

. . . .

As the wheel of the year spun ever forward, the ancient Celts celebrated four Fire Festivals to mark the changing of the seasons: Imbolg (the beginning of spring), Beltaine (the beginning of summer), Lúnasa (the beginning of the harvest season), and Samhain (the end of the harvest season).

The high holy day of Beltaine marked a time when the boundaries between the human and supernatural worlds thinned and people needed to protect themselves, their homes, their fields, and their flocks against enchantments and evil energies. The people would herd their cattle between two great bonfires to bless them and protect them against evil and disease before sending them up to the hills to their summer pastures.

Just as at Samhain, Beltaine Eve was a Spirit Night and the walls between the worlds were thin. For Druids and other magical folk, it was a good time for divinations, incantations, and taking trips to the Otherworld of the Faeries and the ancestors, to bring back a message or simply to have an experience. As you will learn from this tale, Druids had to be highly trained to be able to move between the worlds.

✸

Cailyn was fourteen years old and had just begun her Druid studies. One morning in early spring, she sat cross-legged on the ground in a dark little hut lit only by a single candle and the small fire burning in the round, central hearth ringed by stones. It was a beautiful day outside, and through the walls she could hear the villagers laughing and joking as they cut fresh boughs of birch and hawthorn to decorate the fronts of their houses. She also heard children shrieking in glee as they went out in gangs to gather primroses and lay them across the thresholds to keep mischievous Faeries from coming inside.

"It's not fair!" Cailyn said out loud to no one in particular.

She was now a student in the Druid college, which was all her grandfather's idea. "I always wanted a Druid scholar in the family!" he would say. And because Cailyn was good at memorizing things, she was now apprenticed to Devin, the chief poet of their tribe.

"You have to learn your *oghams,*" Devin had said just that morning. "River ogham and tree ogham and pig ogham and cow ogham. I want you to memorize them all by tomorrow!"

"Tomorrow!" wailed Cailyn. "But tomorrow is Beltaine and I . . ."

"No more complaints!" Devin said, gathering up her staff and the hem of her long white robe as she swished out the door.

Cailyn's little sister Eren was just outside, hiding behind an elder tree, waiting for Devin to leave. As soon as Devin was out of sight, Eren rushed in the door, hoping not to be seen.

"Can't you come outside and help me gather rowan branches? This is the one night of the year when they have power. Do you want to miss that?" Eren pleaded. She held several twigs of rowan that she had already broken off, and she was going to bind them with red thread to make equal-armed solar crosses that would protect the house and barn.

Cailyn sighed. "It's *so* unfair. Just because I am the oldest sister, I have to study reading and writing and memorize stories and alphabets! All so I can grow up to be a Druid. Who wants to be a Druid, anyway? I'd rather be running barefoot through the fields, like you, and having fun with everyone else!"

"I know," said Eren. "Let's escape this dreary hut. If you put on your cape and pull up your hood, nobody will recognize you. It will be so much fun to fool the elders and jump the flames, just like everybody else! Oh, please come outside. It can't be right that you are forced to stay inside this dark, dusty place on Beltaine Eve!"

Cailyn rubbed her chin and thought for a minute, glancing out the open door, seeing warm Sun glistening on thick green grass that was dot-ted with flowers. "You're right! Let's get out of here!" she finally said. And away they went, with hoods raised so their faces were hidden and they wouldn't attract attention.

There was a hill outside the village where all the great Fire Festivals were celebrated with bonfires and feasting. For the tribe, Beltaine was one of the most important days of the year. Devin had kept her eye on the local hawthorn trees, and the moment she found the first tree in bloom, she went through the village loudly announcing that Beltaine had arrived!

"You see, one of the jobs of a Druid is to keep a careful watch on the local hawthorn trees," she had explained to Cailyn that very morning. "The trees know when it is warm enough to send the cattle up to the hills. They tell us by their flowering."

Preparations were under way to build two sacred bonfires made from nine sacred woods, and a third fire just for dancing around. Nine strong men had removed all metal from their bodies, so as not to offend the Faeries, and walked deep into the forest to search for fallen branches and boughs.*

Everywhere, women and girls were preparing bannocks to be used in their land blessings, and the sweet, yeasty smell of these round, flat, oatcakes hung in the air. Young men and warriors sat cross-legged on the grass, sharpening their swords and tools on whetstones and coating them with goose grease to protect them from the damp. The whole tribe was preparing for summer.

"Let's pick all the yellow flowers we can find to decorate Mamaí's May bush," Cailyn suggested.

Mamaí and the aunts always made a May bush—a small tree decorated

---

*According to tradition, wood dropped from a tree is freely given for human use. The Faeries despise iron, so any harvesting or trimming must be done by hand, without the use of a knife—though some say a bone, crystal, or flint knife can be used without giving offense. The nine sacred woods are alder, ash, birch, elm, hazel, oak, rowan, willow, and yew.

like the Sun, with yellow flowers, yellow strips of cloth, and eggs dyed yellow—for the tribe every year. The girls were happy to contribute. They bent to their task, searching out marsh marigolds, buttercups, dandelions, and primroses, trying hard not to stain their clothing. It felt good to be out in the bright sunshine, with the warm grass between their toes.

"This is so much better than being trapped inside on a warm spring day!" Cailyn exclaimed. "But I don't want Mamaí to see us. She will just make me go back to Devin's hut. We can leave the flowers by the door of our house, and she will think the Faeries brought them!"

"That's a good plan!" agreed Eren.

The Sun was already starting to go down behind the hill where the sacred fires would be lit.

"I'm starving!" Eren exclaimed.

They hadn't eaten since morning, and freshly baked bannocks sat cooling outside every door. There was a neat stack of the oatcakes on a stone outside of Mamaí and Dadaí's roundhouse, too.

"I don't think they will miss just one," said Cailyn, looking around and seeing nobody about. They deposited the flowers by the entrance and in exchange took the topmost bannock from the pile.

Now it was nearly dusk, that magical, liminal time between day and night. Three huge piles of wood were in place at the top of the hill, ready to be lit. Two men kneeled on the ground next to one of the piles, working to strike a flame using a fire drill made out of two pieces of oak. Household hearths were being doused so that every family could rekindle their home fire with embers from the same sacred flames.

Cailyn and Eren were easily able to sneak up the hill, hoods raised, munching their bannock, and watching all the activity. Darkness was falling fast, like a dark-blue star-sprinkled curtain, as every family made their way up the hill. Family groups were claiming their spots for the night, laying down their plaid blankets, baskets of food, and jugs of mead.* One person from each clan walked quietly into the surrounding

---

*Mead is a fermented beverage made from honey.

forest to leave an offering of bannock and cheese for the Land Spirits and the Sidhe.

One of the three pyres was lit. Devin's husband, Diarmuid, who was also a Druid, sang the incantation that blessed the sacred flames. He was wearing a long, feathered cape that was symbolic of his rank, and Cailyn and Eren thought he looked very distinguished. Diarmuid dropped pats of butter and fragrant herbs into the fire as an offering. Then the grandmothers and grandfathers began circling the fire, uttering prayers that the flames would carry to the skies.

Soon everyone was dancing and singing. Tadhg, the local piper, played his uilleann pipes and wooden flute by turns as the people picked up their feet. Cailyn and Eren longed to join in but kept to the shadows so they wouldn't get caught, staring in envy as their friends and all the other young people of the village leaped the flames for luck. The higher their leaping, the higher the grain would grow!

As dawn drew near and the flames sank to embers, young women hoping for husbands stepped gracefully through the coals. Pregnant women also walked through the ashes to ensure an easy labor, and newborn babies were handed back and forth across the glowing coals from mothers to grandmothers and back as a blessing.

Finally, as the Sun began rising it was time to light the second and third pyres and to pass the cows between them. The fires had to be so close together that a white cow would have her fur singed brown. The men of the village joined forces to herd the animals between the flames as purification, in preparation for their journey to the summer pastures.

The women and children ran back to their houses to gather up bundles of blankets, clothing, and food for their journey to follow the herds, while the men scooped up ashes and embers and carried them out to the fields to scatter through the corn rows as a blessing. Heads of families took their bannocks out to the furrows, broke them up, and left pieces behind as offerings to appease the crows, eagles, ravens, and foxes who might harm the herds and fields.

Tadgh, the piper, kept playing all the while. Soon he would be leading the procession of animals and people as they made their way up to the hills.

By now the Sun was well above the horizon. "Oh no!" said Eren. "Mamaí will be looking for me now!"

"You better go find her," sighed Cailyn.

She knew that Devin would be looking for her, too. She might even get her ears boxed for disappearing without permission.

Cailyn and Eren rose stiffly from the dew-damp grass, brushing bits of green, sticks, and leaves off their tunics. They were so intent on their task that they didn't even see the sandaled feet standing right in front of them!

"Devin!" Cailyn squeaked, once she finally noticed who it was.

"Uh oh," said Eren, knowing that their goose was cooked.

Devin grabbed Eren by the arm, and none too gently. "Go home to your mother. She has been looking for you all night!" she said in a gruff voice.

Eren rose quickly and scuttled off in the direction of her parents' roundhouse.

"I have a few choice words for you, Cailyn," Devin said, leaning on her staff and making her face into a twisted mask. "I was planning to take you to the hills for a very important lesson today. I had no intention of leaving you in the dark, memorizing your alphabets on Beltaine!"

Cailyn was very tired from being up all night and felt like crying. "I am so sorry. I was a fool," she said, humiliated and ashamed and not quite able to meet her teacher's eyes.

"Well, staying up another day and night will be your penance. Now come with me!" Devin commanded.

Cailyn was very hungry, tired, and damp, but she didn't say a word. Instead, she fell meekly in step behind Devin. Then she realized they were leaving the village—but in the opposite direction from everyone else!

"Where are we headed?" she asked.

"Do you remember that old solitary hawthorn tree on top of Faery Hill?" Devin asked.

"Yes," Cailyn replied. "I have been told all my life never to go near it."

"That's where we are going," Devin said. "Just you and me and nobody else. This is what I had planned to show you on this special day."

They reached the hilltop and sat down in the thick grass and heather. The Faery tree was just a few feet away. Devin reached into her pouch and pulled out a piece of bannock and a wedge of cheese.

"Go ahead and leave these at the base of the tree," Devin said, pointing to a little hollow between two roots. It looked like a bare space where offerings had been left before.

Cailyn rose, approaching the tree slowly, feeling a mixture of dread and curiosity. All her life she had been warned to never disturb the Faery hawthorn! She gently slipped the offering between the roots and quickly returned to her teacher.

Devin spoke, "One day you will be a Druid for your community. There are things you need to know to preserve good relations between the people, and between the people and the Good Neighbors—the Sidhe.

"First, the Good Neighbors like to steal butter. To prevent this, anyone entering a house where churning is going on *must* offer to help."

"My mamaí always makes a wreath of clover, balm of the warrior's wound,* vervain, and dill and binds it with ivy. She puts it under the milk pail to keep the Faeries from stealing the milk, or she hangs it on the barn door," said Cailyn.

"Sensible practice," said Devin. "Such a wreath doesn't as much keep them away as keep them distracted. You see, they love greenery above all things, and they are fascinated by the bound-up herbs. That's also the reason we decorate the front of our houses with green boughs of birch and lay primroses and yellow flowers across the thresholds and around our sacred well. The Faeries are so entranced by the blossoms that they won't bother to enter the house. And on that subject, there is a flower they love so much that they will actually follow it into the house, which is never a good idea. You can't imagine the kind of mischief they get into when that happens . . . Do you know which flower that is?"

---

*Balm of the warrior's wound is another folk name for St. John's wort.

"Oh yes!" said Cailyn. "The blooming hawthorn!"

"Correct!" said Devin. "This is why we *never* bring blooming hawthorn into our homes."

Devin continued with her recitation of lore.

"There is a type of Moon Faery, called a *Lunantisidhe,* that guards the blackthorn bushes. You must never cut a blackthorn stick on Beltaine or Samhain or you will have very bad luck.* And you must *never* cut down a Faery tree like this one," Devin added, pointing to the solitary hawthorn before them, "because that will bring sickness or death to you and your cattle!"

"Is that because we would be destroying the Faeries' home?" Cailyn asked.

"Yes. A solitary hawthorn marks an entrance to the land of the Faeries, especially if there is a water source nearby. These trees must also be protected because they are important for making medicine—the flowers, young leaves, and berries are a tonic for the heart, and the berries simmered with apples and honey make a syrup for the cough."

"So really we are protecting the tree, the Faeries, *and* the people," said Cailyn.

"Correct!" said Devin. "The same thing applies to elder trees, whose flowers and berries are good for fevers and sweats. You must always encourage the people to respect the Sidhe. Every household should leave out a bowl of milk or fresh water for them at night. And if any food falls on the floor it should not be eaten because it belongs to the spirits."

"And as you know, it is bad luck to trespass on a Faery fort,† especially after dark. It's an insult to the Good Neighbors if you disturb such a place. And all care must be taken with them when you're building a new house. Before digging the foundation, you must leave a piece of sod

---

*Blackthorn sticks are cut to make *shillelaghs* (*shuh-LAY-lees*), a type of club that is used as a weapon.

†Faery forts are old circular embankments, often made of stone, found in many places in the countryside of Ireland—all that's left of fortified structures built in ancient times.

from the western side upside down overnight. If the sod is untouched in the morning, that means the house is not disturbing a Faery track. But if the sod is turned over again, you will need to build in a different location.

"One more thing," Devin cautioned. "When you throw wash water out of the house, you must always warn the Faeries first, because very bad luck will follow those who do not respect the Sidhe.

"Now I have one last lesson for you," Devin said, using her Druid staff to pull herself to her feet. She gestured for Cailyn to follow as she approached the Faery tree. Then, using the butt end of her staff, she struck a nearby rock very hard, three times.

Cailyn's world went suddenly milk white. There was nothing for her to see or feel other than a luminous white haze. Then, as the haze slowly melted away like morning mist, Cailyn found that she was floating in the sky! Looking below, she could see fields, villages, and cattle. But looking up, instead of sky she saw waves of water, as if she were under a vast lake or the sea.

Suddenly she felt herself falling. Down and down she went until she landed on the softest, greenest grass she had ever seen. Twinkling in between the blades of grass were fragrant flowers of every hue. Blooming bushes and trees were all around, filled with colorful birds singing their hearts out in a majestic chorus. Every blooming tree and bush was covered with the most beautiful and tempting fruit . . . everything was in perfect balance and harmony . . . it was so lovely!

And then she heard three sharp knocks, and Devin's voice. "Come back now!"

"What was that!" Cailyn exclaimed, rubbing her eyes. "Where have I been?"

Devin replied, smiling, "You have just visited Tír na nÓg, the land of the Faeries. There is no better place to enter there than from the base of a Faery tree, and no time better than Beltaine or Samhain.* I am very glad

*The actual dates are May 11 (Old Beltaine) and November 11 (Old Samhain).

that you made it there and back safely! You must not have eaten anything in that place, because if you had, I would not have been able to bring you home for seven years! You must not tell anyone about this. Only when you have your own Druid apprentice may you share the secrets of the Faery tree!"

"I promise!" said Cailyn. "Truly."

And it wasn't until many years later, when she was a professor at the Druid college, that she finally took her own student on a very special journey to the land of the Faeries, while standing under the hawthorn tree.

❧ THE BELTAINE BANNOCK ❧

Long ago, on Beltaine, people would bake a large bannock—a round, flat oatcake—and carry it out to the fields. They broke off sections of it, one by one, giving each as an offering to an animal that might threaten the crops and herds, such as crows, ravens, eagles, and foxes, asking the animal to leave the flocks and fields alone. The proper way to do this was to throw a piece of bannock behind you in the name of the animal you were petitioning. You might say, "This is for you, Raven. Please spare my corn." Or "This is for you, Fox. Please leave my chickens alone." And so on.

²/₃ cup coarsely ground oats, plus a handful or two for
    kneading and baking

1 pinch baking soda

1 pinch sea salt

2 teaspoons butter or lard, melted

1 cup hot water

Combine the oats, the salt, and the baking soda in a bowl and stir together.

Make a well in the center of the oat mixture.

Pour the melted butter and hot water into the well and stir until a stiff batter forms.

Cover a large wooden cutting board with a scattering of ground oats and empty the batter onto the board.

Coat your hands with ground oats and then knead the batter into a ball of dough.

Use a rolling pin or a glass bottle to roll out the dough to ½-inch thickness. Sprinkle the dough with ground oats.

Grease a griddle or cast-iron pan and warm it over medium heat.

Cook the bannock until the edges are curled and slightly toasted, for about 10 to 15 minutes, then flip and cook the other side. If the bottom burns that means the stove is too hot!

In ancient times, the bannock would have been rolled thin and stuck to a sheepskin, which would be placed on a wooden stretcher near the fire until the bread was toasted. It was considered very unlucky and an offense to the Faeries for iron to touch the bannock if it was intended as a bread for ritual purposes.

***

Learn the
Tree Ogham Alphabet

The ancient Irish created oghams, or alphabets, by associating each letter with a word. The tree ogham, in which each letter corresponds to a tree, was used by Druids and is possibly the oldest, original ogham. There were many others, such as the bird ogham, color ogham, dog ogham, cow ogham, and so on. Some say these oghams were secret codes that Druids used to communicate with each other, and others say they were a device to make it easier to memorize lists of things. Maybe they were both!

Beltaine is intimately associated with trees, probably because they come into full leaf and flower around the time of this festival. So, the Druidic tree ogham is the perfect alphabet to learn at this time of year. Let's take a look.

THE LETTERS OF THE TREE OGHAM

Letter		Name	Associated Tree/Plant
B	⊢	beith *(beth)*	birch
L	⊨	luis *(lush)*	rowan
F	⊫	fearn *(FYE-hrn)*	alder
S	≣	saille *(SAHL-yeh)*	willow
N	≣	nion *(nyun)*	ash
H	⊣	uath *(OO-ath)*	hawthorn
D	⫤	dair *(dar)*	oak
T	⊒	tinne *(TIN-nyuh)*	holly
C	⊟	coll *(kol)*	hazel
Q	≣	quert *(QOO-ehrt)*	apple
M	⅄	muin *(mwin)*	vine
G	⚡	gort *(gort)*	ivy
P or Ng	≢	ngetal *(NYEH-dul)*	reed

THE LETTERS OF THE TREE OGHAM
(continued)

Letter	Name	Associated Tree/Plant
Ss	straif *(straf)*	blackthorn
R	ruis *(rush)*	elder
A	ailm *(AL-um or AL-uv)*	fir or pine
O	onn *(uhn)*	furze or gorse
U	úr *(oor)*	heather
E	edad *(ETH-ath)*	aspen
I	idad *(ITH-ath)*	yew

You can read more about the ancient tree ogham and its magical uses in my book *A Druid's Herbal of Sacred Tree Medicine* (2008).

❋

Make Your Own Maypole

The Maypole is a British May Day tradition. First you will need a straight tree, traditionally a birch, of about sixteen feet. See if you can find a tree that has been knocked down by a storm. You can also cut one down; look for a thickly wooded area where the trees could use some thinning. Or you can use a live tree with its lower branches removed. Some people resort to using PVC pipe when they don't have access to a tree.

Dig a hole in the ground, deep enough that the tree will stand in it and just wide enough for the tree's trunk to fit in. A three-foot-deep hole that is about four inches wider than the tree's trunk should work. Keep the dirt you dig out handy, as well as some rocks, to pack into the hole and secure the tree once you set it in place.

Before you erect the pole, make a wreath of flowers to go on the top. Fresh-blooming hawthorn is traditional, but any flowers will do. Use silk flowers if need be. Bind the flowers to the wreath with ribbons and ivy. Then hang the wreath from the top of the pole.

You will also need to make a wire wreath to hang the ribbons from and secure it about one foot from the top of the pole. Do this by winding wire around the top of the tree. Secure the wire with nails and staples (or more wire, if you're working with a live tree as nails could hurt the tree). Cut one ribbon for each dancer. Each ribbon should be about twice the height of the pole. Then tie all the ribbons in a circle around the wire wreath.

Now that the flower and ribbon wreaths are in place, you can

A simple Maypole ready to be danced around

erect the pole. You'll need helpers! Set the base of the pole in the prepared hole and secure it with rocks and dirt.

When the pole is ready, the dancers can get into position. Ideally, you'll have an even number of dancers. Every other dancer will move sunwise (clockwise), and every other dancer will move counterclockwise, each holding a ribbon. The group going sunwise starts with their ribbons held up, so they can go over the person they face, and the group going counterclockwise starts with their ribbons down, so they can pass under. As each dancer encounters a person coming at them from the opposite direction, they change their ribbon to the next position: up and then down, up and then down.

With music, singing, drumming, or chanting, begin the dance, with the dancers going under and then over the people coming at them, holding their ribbon firmly, until they are circling very close to the pole. I am always impressed when a Maypole dance makes an

*Maypole dancers
and revelers.
Photos by Lady Tiana Mirapae.*

even woven design, but if just one person breaks the pattern, it ends up with a more "original" look—not a bad thing!

The dance should be spirited and fun, with lots of laughter. The closer the dancers get to the pole, the faster everything moves. Musicians take note! Eventually the dancers will start bumping into each other and the ribbons will become too short to maneuver. At this point, everyone should tie their ribbon to the pole, and each dancer (still singing, chanting, or toning) should put their hand on the pole and think of their wish for the coming year.

Once the pole is wound and done, it is time to welcome new babies, newly married couples, and anyone with an achievement or declaration to step up to the pole and make their announcement to the community.

❋

Make Your Own May Bush

The Irish traditionally celebrate May Day with a May bush, a bush or tree decorated with lights, streamers, and dyed eggs. The decorated bush is set up in front of a home or in a communal area. In ancient times it was set up by adults, but in modern times children are usually the focus of the activity. "Long life, a pretty wife, and a candle for the May bush"—that's the magical incantation to be proclaimed as children gather decorations for their May bush.

The "bush" is traditionally a hawthorn tree, though yellow-flowered gorse may also be used and any small tree will do. The decorations are yellow: yellow flowers, yellow ribbons, yellow-dyed eggs (emptied of their yolks), all in honor of the Sun. In ancient times, there might have been candles attached to the tree; in modern times, Christmas lights will do.

May bushes are designed to be very visible because they protect the house and land from the mischief of the Faeries. Good crops and a healthy milk yield are thus ensured. The fate of the bush is tied to

*A simple May bush.
Photo by Deirdre
Wadding.*

the luck of the house or the community—it is very bad luck if the bush is stolen or knocked down.

In days gone by, the whole village would feast and dance around a bonfire and the candle-lit May bush to celebrate the season. That custom most likely comes from a time when fires were lit on hilltops to frighten away predators and protect the herds. Indeed, sometimes the May bush itself is burned on Beltaine (May Day) Eve.

If you'd like to make your own May bush but can't manage a whole tree, try making a May bough—a smaller version of the custom, in which you decorate a tree branch and hang it outside your house.

---※---

Beltaine Magic: Planting Seeds

Beltaine is a time when the boundary between the worlds thins and wild magic seeps through to our world. You can take part in the powerful forces now sweeping over the land with a simple gardening ritual like this one adapted from my friend Shawn Moore's gardening magic:

- Procure yourself some vegetable seeds. Bless them.
- Pick a good growing spot outside, in the very womb of Mother Earth. Make sure it gets good light. Bless the spot, and give thanks to it.
- Place the seeds into the earth in your chosen spot, as deeply and as far apart as they need (you can look up planting instructions online), and then carefully fold the earth back together with your fingers.
- Every few days, add the magical elixir of life we call "water" to the spot where you planted your seeds.
- Keep an eye on your planting spot. In a week or so, you will see your magic come forth in the shape of newborn seedlings, sprung forth from Mother Earth.

A little Beltaine magic

➤ Keep feeding your seedlings the elixir of life, and protect them from invaders who would strangle and feed off their energy, such as weeds, insects, and animals.

➤ When your vegetables have ripened, remove them, give thanks, and consume them, placing all you do not consume back into the earth so the remains may feed, renew, and give life.

Summer Solstice

Longest day,

Shortest night,

Time to light our fire bright,

To write on parchment

What we seek to banish,

And give it to the Fire,

And watch it vanish!

To write on parchment

What we desire,

And give it to Fire!

Fire takes our wishes high,

Carried to spirits in the sky.

To the flames our thanks

We utter,

Offering herbs and

Pats of butter. *

---

*It's traditional to give fire the things that it likes, such as butter, oil, ghee, whiskey, dried herbs, beeswax, and incense.

When the embers
Start to lower,
We leap the flame.
As high our leaping,
So high the grain!

We honor Fire in the sky
And give thanks to Sun and Stars.

We also remember what's
Deep underground,
And give our thanks
To the hot, molten Earth.

Thank you, Fire!

7

KUPALNOCKA AND THE MAGICAL FERN FLOWER

A Polish Tale for the Summer Solstice (June 20/21/22)

················ **Key Figures and Terms** ················

Gods, Goddesses, Spirits, and Magical Beings:

Domovoi (*DOME-oh-voy*)—a spirit of the household who protects the family and house.

Polish Words to Know:

babcia (*BOB-cha*)—grandmother.

Kupalnocka (*KOO-pahl-NOHT-zka*)—Kupala Night, a festival of sacred fire and sacred water, kind of like a Polish Valentine's Day.

pierogi (*pi-ROW-gee*)—small dough dumplings stuffed with a filling.

Tata (*TAH-tah*)—an informal name for a father, like "Dad."

wianek (*VIA-neck*)—wreath.

··

Kupala's Night, or Kupalnocka, is a Slavonic celebration of Midsummer, or the Summer Solstice. The name Kupala comes from the slavonic word for "to bathe." The rituals associated with this festival involve both fire and water. Fire is related to the Sun and the masculine energies, and water is related to the Moon and feminine forces. When these two elements come together it symbolizes the union of the divine masculine and the divine feminine. This day also marks the turning of the Sun to winter, when the days first begin to become shorter.

On this night songs about love, romance, and marriage are sung. There is dancing around the bonfire, symbolic of passion, and bathing naked in rivers and lakes, or even just rolling in dewy grass, to enhance one's personal beauty.

Young women make wreaths, symbolic of their intelligence and purity, and throw them into the water for young men to catch. The girls pay careful attention to the magical properties of the flowers and herbs they use to make their wreaths. Couples wander off into the night to search for the magical fern flower that blooms only on this night. When found, it bestows prosperity, luck, and power.

✳

It was the night before Kupalnocka, and Ewa, who was twelve, Halina, who was six, and Justyn, who was eleven, were sad because Tata and Mama were fighting again. It was always over the same thing, Tata would say that he had to leave and sell things in a market far away, and then Mama would be left alone to care for the farm, the animals, and the children. That always made her angry and sad.

Mama still had their big sister, Julita, to help with the chores, but Julita was being courted by Feliks, the blacksmith's son, and she would very likely be married soon. Where would that leave poor Mama? She would be all on her own for half of the year with a big farm to manage!*

Their grandmother, whom the children called Babcia, was the village wise woman. She was the person everyone went to when they had a problem. Because she had lived so many years, she knew which cures worked best for sick babies or ailing goats and chickens. She was someone they

---

*The young people's names are pronounced as follows: Ewa *(EH-vah)*, Halina *(CHAH-lee-nah)*, Justyn *(YOO-styn)*, Julita *(ee-OOH-lee-tah)*, and Feliks *(FEH-leeks)*.

could turn to with questions about life, such as how to make a good marriage or ensure a bountiful harvest.

Babcia knew which plants to burn to protect the fields from hail, and
which herbs to hang in the window or over the door to repel evil spirits.
She even had a collection of roots and herbs you could wear to increase
your luck and personal power!

Ewa, Halina, and Justyn decided to walk to Babcia's house to ask for
advice on how to help Mama and Tata stop quarreling. When they got
there, they found Babcia in her garden, dressed in a long green embroidered skirt and a snowy white apron. She wore a flowered shawl on her
shoulders that was mostly white and was speckled all over with red roses,
green leaves, and bluebells. The ends of the shawl tucked into her belt,
and she had a red-flowered kerchief of a different color and pattern on her
head. She was a riot of color and fit right in with the blooming herbs and
ferns and flowers that grew all around her little thatched house. As she
walked, her white cat, Maleńka (whose name meant "little one"), wound
around and through her legs, purring.

Babcia's house was a riot of color, too. The walls outside were yellow, and the walls inside were blue, and all the walls had flowers painted
on them.

"I made my house like this to keep the Faeries happy," she would say.
"They think of my home as just another section of the garden, which is
good and proper and just as it should be. Because when I call on them for
help, I want them to feel perfectly at home here!" And nobody could argue
with that.

Hidden in one of her flower beds, Babcia had a small stone altar where
she would always leave a portion of her baking for the Faeries. She had
another altar in the corner of the house that she kept just for them, with
a plate for food offerings and a green glass vase that always held a fresh
flower in spring, summer, and fall. In winter she would keep a branch of
fresh pine in the glass, just for the enjoyment of the Domovoi, the household spirit.

On this particular day, Babcia was busy gathering herbs and flowers in a huge woven basket, because anything picked on Kupala Eve would have special powers. Kupala is the time when the powers of nature (the above-ground ones, anyway) are strongest and the land is filled with a radiant energy that pushes the harvest to its height. Herbs to promote fertility and love are at the peak of their power at this time, and plants for healing are suffused with special magic. Ewa, Halina, and Justyn were always a little in awe of Babcia and all that she knew.

"Hello, children!" Babcia called out gaily when she saw them approaching her gate. "How is everyone at your house? Are they keeping well?"

Babcia was very perceptive. She could tell by their faces that the children were troubled. "Why don't you come inside, and I will make you a nice cup of my special chocolate brew. I already have peppermint hot cocoa ready to go on the stove!"

The children's eyes lit up. Somehow Babcia always knew when they were coming—sometimes even before they knew it themselves! And she always had a special treat ready for them when they appeared at her door. Maleńka led the way, with her tail raised like a flag, as they all trooped into the colorful little cottage.

The children told Babcia about Tata and Mama as she whisked together peppermint tea, fresh milk from her goats, and honey on top of the wood-stove. Then she broke a chocolate bar into little pieces and dropped them into the hot liquid, whisking it some more. The children's mouths watered as they went to the cupboard, carefully took out four mugs, and set them on the wooden table.

Babcia heard their complaints and then told them just what to do.

"I will take you out to the field to gather St. John's wort," she said. "You must hang a bunch over every entrance and weave it into crowns for everyone in the family to wear. Make sure your parents wear them, too. That herb, especially when picked this day, will drive all evil thoughts and spirits from your home.

"Next you must pick bundles of thyme—it grows in the kitchen garden behind the house. Make a very strong tea of it and use it to wash your floors. You should also stuff some into every pillow in the house.

"I will find you oregano, wormwood, and mugwort, too, to put into your pillows. Those herbs keep bad spirits and sadness away. And I want you to go into the forest and cut fresh birch branches with new leaves on them, and also ferns and wild forest flowers. You should hang those all over the house, both inside and out, and especially over the windows and doors."

Sipping her delicious brew, the children took in her advice. Then, when they had finished, they wiped their mouths, rinsed their mugs, and followed Babcia and Maleńka to the field out back. There they gathered all the herbs and flowers she had suggested. Then they went into the forest and, again, gathered all the plants she had named. Soon their arms were filled with birch, ferns, wood violets, St. John's wort, purple loosestrife, chamomile, speedwell, mullein, yarrow, thyme, oregano, wormwood, mugwort, and cinquefoil, and it was time to leave. Babcia bid them each farewell with a warm hug and a kiss.

When they got home, there was Mama, sitting on a stool in a dark corner, looking sad. She had a brown woolen shawl over her head and shoulders, and her brown skirt and black apron echoed her mood.

"Why are you so unhappy?" Justyn asked.

"Tata has just left again. He went to the village to buy a new bridle," she said quietly.

It did seem strange that Tata would leave on the eve of the Kupala festival.

"Where is Julita?" Ewa asked. Her big sister should have been at home, helping Mama make the family's special *pierogi,* filled with sour cherry preserves from the trees in the garden, for the celebration.

"She is with her friends making flower wreaths down by the river," Mama answered. "They're going to throw them into the river tonight, at the festival, and Julita hopes that Feliks will catch hers when it washes near the riverbank. Then everyone in the village will see that they belong to each other . . . and then she will leave us!" Mama added with a little sob.

The children dropped their bundles of herbs and branches onto the big wooden supper table.

"See what we have brought!" said Halina. "Don't be sad! Babcia told us what to gather to magically protect our house and family!" She put her arms around Mama as Ewa and Justyn went to look for scissors, nails, string, and a hammer. Soon the house was hung with flowers and fresh branches, both inside and out. Then the children set to work making flower and herb wreaths for every member of the family to wear, including Julita, just in case she was too busy to make her own.

Ewa put thyme on the stove to simmer and then mopped the floors with the tea, as Babcia had instructed. Justyn and Halina stuffed magical plants into all the pillows, and Halina convinced Mama to change into a red embroidered skirt with a snowy white blouse and apron, a necklace of red beads, and a bright green shawl. "Wearing bright colors always makes you feel better, Mama," Halina said.

At last, the Sun was setting and it was time to attend the village bonfire. Everyone in the area would attend because the fire was lit to drive evil forces away from the village, and if you didn't show up, people might think you were evil, too!

They packed boiled eggs, bread, and cheese into baskets and walked down the lane to the village. It was a warm evening, and a dusky light shone through branches of the apple trees on both sides of the little dirt road. When they got to the river, they saw young men and women bathing there, because on this night the waters were filled with magical powers to make the body and soul alluring. Then it would be easy to attract love, a good marriage, or a good relationship.

On a hillside nearby, they could see some people steadying a large wheel made of grass and straw. A man from the village brought a torch and held it to the wheel so it caught fire. Once the flames were well under way, they let it go and the fiery wheel rolled down the hill, gaining speed rapidly. A crowd of people followed the wheel, shouting and hooting as it careened its way down the slope. Finally, it hit the river with a hiss and then slowly sank.

"Why do they do that?" Halina asked.

"Because today is the day of the Summer Solstice, the longest day of the year. After this night the Sun will be in decline," said Mama. "This is how we honor the Sun's descent into winter."

"Already?" Halina asked.

"Oh yes," said Mama. "Haven't you noticed how, after Kupalnocka, the days start getting shorter?"

Babcia saw them approaching. She waved as she came toward them and then hugged each one. She took Mama by the hand.

"Irena," she said (that was Mama's name), "you must walk into the river and wet your feet, face, and hands. And look who I found standing by the bonfire."

It was Tata!

Babcia took Tata by the hand and put his hand into Mama's. "Now you must *both* go into the river and bathe in its magical powers!"

Tata and Mama looked into each other's eyes, and Mama looked like she might cry. The children watched as their father and mother took off their shoes and socks. Tata rolled up his pant legs and Mama hitched the ends of her skirt into her belt, and they went, hand in hand, down to the river.

Then over the hill and to the river came Julita and her friends, each of them clutching a large wreath made of wildflowers and grasses. The young men of the village were watching them closely, because each was trying to memorize which wreath belonged to the woman he liked best.

Every young woman had a beautiful crown of flowers on her head, and so did the young men. The women released their wreaths to the water current, and then the men ran along the riverbank, trying to keep up with the wreath of their sweetheart and hoping to catch it when it came near shore. Some of the men even jumped into the water and swam out to retrieve a particular wreath.

"Babcia, why are they swimming after those rings of flowers?" Halina asked.

"A *wianek* holds a lot of magic" Babcia said. "You can tell the worth of a relationship by the way it floats down the river. If a girl's wreath floats quickly back to shore and her young man easily grabs it, they will have a happy, carefree union. If the wianek floats smoothly and encounters no obstacles or snags, they will have a love with no quarrels. But if the wianek spins or gets tangled up, it means grief and problems. And the worst sign of all is if the wianek sinks—that could even mean death!"

Mama and Tata clambered back to shore and went over to the huge bonfire to dry off and get warm. Gaily dressed women were dancing in a ring around the pyre, singing songs about love and marriage. In between the dances, boys and girls would make running leaps over the flames, whooping and shouting, banishing bad luck and driving out the last demons of winter with each bold jump.

When the fire was a bit lower, couples began jumping the flames together, holding hands. By leaping the fire in unison, they were demonstrating their compatibility and guaranteeing each other love and faithfulness.

Now the young women who had flung their wreaths into the river returned. Each was holding the hand of an earnest-looking young man. The young men looked very proud of themselves because they had each ensured a future love or even a wife.

Julita and Feliks came toward the family, smiling. Julita reached into her basket and pulled out a large bowl, glazed in blue and white and covered with a linen cloth. "I made these for you this afternoon at my friend's house," she said proudly, handing the bowl to her mother. It was full of sour cherry pierogi, sprinkled with golden sugar!

"I even have a bowl of yogurt to go with them," Julita added, pulling out another bowl covered with a cloth and a large wooden serving spoon.

Ewa took the basket and put both bowls back in it. "I will add this to our evening picnic," she said. Then she and Justyn and Halina began looking for a good spot to spread the family blanket for everyone to sit on and enjoy their evening meal.

"I don't think we will be joining you for supper. Julita and I are going into the forest to seek the magical fern flower!" Feliks declared.

Babcia pulled Mama and Tata aside. "You both should go into the forest and look for the magical fern flower, too," she whispered.

"But we haven't done that since we were teenagers!" Mama protested, blushing.

"I know! It's about time, don't you think?" Babcia answered with a wink.

"Irena," Tata said, "won't you come to the woods with me to seek the magical fern flower?"

Mama smiled. "Yes," she answered. And off they went.

"What is the fern flower?" Justyn asked.

Babcia replied, "The magical fern flower, if you can find it, blooms *exactly* at midnight on the Summer Solstice. If you discover it, a beam of light will shine and you will see a great treasure hidden on that very spot. That treasure will bring you wealth, happiness, and love."

"That's silly," said Halina. "Ferns don't have flowers. Everyone knows that!"

"That is where the magic comes in," said Babcia with a smile. "On this night, many wonderful things can happen. Trees can even speak and move. And couples who go into the forest together can renew or discover their love and purpose."

"I still don't get it," said Halina, shaking her head. She was, after all, only six.

The next morning, Tata and Mama came home looking radiant and happy, even if their clothes were a little rumpled and muddy from being in the forest all night. And after that, Tata rarely went away on trips anymore. "We found the magical fern flower" was all he would say about it.

Julita and Feliks were married at the next full Moon, and that year the harvest was especially rich and fertile.

❦ BABCIA'S MAGICAL PEPPERMINT CHOCOLATE TEA ❧

This recipe makes enough for one extra-large serving or two small servings.

2 cups water

4 teaspoons dried peppermint or 2 peppermint tea bags

4 ounces dark chocolate, broken into small pieces

¼ cup heavy cream

1 tablespoon raw local honey

Whipped cream, for topping, optional

Bring the water to a boil in a small pot, then remove from the heat.

Add the peppermint or the tea bags. Let steep, covered, for about 10 minutes.

Strain out the peppermint (or remove the tea bags) and bring the tea to a simmer (do not boil).

Add the chocolate, then slowly whisk in the cream and honey. Stir until everything is melted and smooth.

Serve with whipped cream on top, if desired.

❦ JULITA'S SOUR CHERRY PIEROGI ❧

If your sour cherries are freshly picked, then before you pit them, clean them: soak them for 20 minutes in enough cold water to cover them, with a tablespoon or two of vinegar added per quart of water, then rinse well. If you don't have sour cherries, you can also make these pierogi with blackberries, raspberries, blueberries, and so on. You'll end up with about fifteen pierogi.

For the filling:

1¼ cups sour cherries

2 tablespoons sugar

2 teaspoons all-purpose flour

For the dough:

1¾ cups all-purpose flour, plus a bit for dusting the table

Dash of sea salt

1 egg, beaten

¼ cup milk (cow, soy, almond, cashew, coconut, rice, oat, hemp, or flax)

¼ cup water

For cooking:

2 quarts water

1 teaspoon sea salt

1 teaspoon vegetable oil

For serving:

¼ cup yogurt or sour cream

2 teaspoons sugar

Prepare the filling:

Remove the pits from the cherries and cut them in half. Place the halved cherries in a bowl and set aside.

Combine the sugar and flour in a bowl and set aside.

Make the dough:

Combine the 1¾ cups of flour and the salt in a large bowl and mix well.

Make a well in the center of the flour. Add the egg to the well and then mix everything together.

Slowly add the milk and keep mixing.

Slowly add the water and keep mixing. Mix until you have a smooth dough.

Scatter a bit of flour over a table or large wooden board. Transfer the dough to the floured work surface.

Use a rolling pin or a glass bottle to roll out the dough to ½ -inch thickness.

Cook the pierogi:

Fill a large pot with the water. Add the salt and oil. Put on the lid and bring the water to a boil.

While you wait for the water to boil, use an upside-down glass or round cookie cutter to cut 3½-inch-wide circles out of the dough. Combine any scraps and roll them out again to repeat this process as needed.

Drop 1 tablespoon of cherries into the middle of each round of dough.

Sprinkle ¼ teaspoon of the sugar and flour mixture over the cherries.

Moisten the edges of each circle with water and fold the circle over to make a half-moon shape. Pinch the edges to seal them.

When you have eight sealed pierogi, drop them into the boiling water. Boil until the dough is very tender, 7 to 10 minutes.

Remove the pierogi from the boiling water with a slotted spoon and slide them onto a plate. Keep going until all your pierogi are cooked.

To serve:

Mix the yogurt and sugar. Use this mixture as a dipping sauce, or pour it over the pierogi.

To keep:

You can freeze the pierogi to keep for later. Just place the uncooked pierogi on a baking sheet, freeze them for 2 hours, then transfer the frozen pierogi to a ziplock bag or plastic container and store in the freezer. They'll keep for 2 to 3 months.

When you want to cook them, just drop the frozen pierogi into boiling water and cook for 8 to 12 minutes, until tender.

This recipe is adapted from Sarah Ozimek, "Blueberry Pierogi," Curious Cusiniere (website), February 19, 2020.

❋

Make a Flower Crown

Flower crowns are easy to make and perfect for celebrating the Summer Solstice, or any other special day.

➤ Cut a bunch of flowers with long stems. Make sure they are all about the same length.

➤ Hold two flowers together, with their blooms pointing in the

*A little girl in a simple
flower crown*

*The author (in the red dress) and her helpers, all wearing
flower crowns at a Beltaine celebration. Photo by Lady Tiana Mirapae.*

same direction. Twist their stems around each other, and bind the stems together with florist's tape or natural twine.

➼ Twist a third flower stem around the second stem, and bind it in place.

➼ Repeat, twisting and binding a new stem to the previous stem, to make a long chain of flowers.

➼ When the chain is the right length for wrapping around your head, twist the two ends together and bind them.

➼ Check the crown for bare spots, and insert more flowers into the chain as needed.

➼ If you like, tie long colorful ribbons to the back of the crown so they hang down your back.

You can use the same technique to make a magical crown of flowers, herbs, grasses, and other plants. Every plant brings its own magic; see the list beginning on page 112.

——————————————— ❋ ———————————————

Make a Magical Kupalnocka Wreath

For your wreath to have real magical power, you should make it yourself. See the list of plants beginning on page 112, and choose plants for your wreath based on the magic you want to create. Float the wreath down a river or onto a lake at dusk on Kupalnocka (the eve of the Summer Solstice). Say a prayer to the water spirits as you release the wreath. And please use only natural ingredients so you don't pollute the water!

➼ Gather supple, bendable branches and vines, such as grapevines, bittersweet vines, long branches of boxwood or rosemary, birch branches with new leaves on them, eucalyptus stems, weeping willow branches, lengths of ivy, and so on.

➼ Form one long, flexible branch into a circle. Tie the ends together with natural twine.

A homemade Kupalnocka wreath.
Photo by Slavinkay.

An image of Kupalnocka Night. Divination on the Wreaths,
by Simon Kozhin—Иван Купала. Гадание на венках.

-》 Weave more branches and woody stems around the branch, passing them over and under and around to hold them in place. Secure the ends as needed with natural twine.

-》 Add fresh greenery to your wreath, again passing it over, under, and around the woody wreath and using twine to secure it as needed.

-》 Finally, weave in any flowers you might be using.

·············· **Magical Properties of Flowers,** ···············
Herbs, Vines, and Woods

Use these plants to make magical wreaths, crowns, and bouquets.

Apple: For innocent, sweet love, roll two pink candles in fresh apple blossom petals and honey on the full Moon. Burn the candles together while chanting, "Love be here, here to stay, the time is now, light the way." Carry a bit of apple tree wood to attract a sweet lover.

Basil: Use the tea to wash the floors and walls to protect your house and family. It attracts customers and repels thieves from a place of business when used as a floor wash or placed in a bowl on the counter or shelf. Rub some basil oil on your forehead as protection when you're in a crowd of people, especially those you do not trust.

Birch: Use the "Lady of the Woods," as birch is known, for cleansing, renewal, and purification and to get organized for a new project. It is the tree of new beginnings. Make a broom of birch twigs with an ash handle, bound with willow, and use it to brush away the old and make room for the new.

Bittersweet: This plant is very protective. Hang bunches upside down by the entrances to your home to protect the house and your family from harmful spirits and people.

Boxwood: Brings courage, enhances magical power, and increases energy, strength, and determination. Use it for cleansing and purification in times of change. Inside your home, place it by a window or on the mantle to drive unwanted spirits from the room. *Caution:* Boxwood is poisonous to dogs, cats, and other small mammals. If you have pets, be sure they cannot reach it.

Chamomile: Hang a wreath of chamomile in your home to protect it from lightning. Sprinkle the flowers around the house and in the bath for courage and protection.

Cinquefoil: Use this herb in the bath to wash away curses. Fill an empty eggshell with the herb, tape it shut, and hide it somewhere in the home to protect the property. It's known as the "helping hand"; keep a pressed leaf (you can preserve it between two pieces of clear shelf paper) in your backpack, taped to your laptop, or somewhere in your bedroom to aid you with your projects.

Cotoneaster: A favorite of the bees, butterflies, birds, and Faeries. It has tiny red berries. Grow it in the garden just to keep the Faeries happy.

Delphinium: Blue delphinium (also known as larkspur) attracts altruism and generosity. It repels ghosts and evil or unfriendly spirits. Hang it in a barn to protect the animals.

Eucalyptus: Creates a protective shield around you when you carry it or keep it in your home. Brings fresh energy to a situation. Soothes regrets, worries, mental exhaustion, and physical or emotional concerns. Place some next to a picture of someone who is sick or next to their jewelry box.

Fennel: Use fennel for healing and protection. Wear it around your neck to repel sorcery.

Fern: For rain making, dip a fern frond in water and shake it around the garden. Fern also attracts protection, good luck, wealth, and health. A thick stand of ferns marks an entrance to the Faery realm.

Ivy: Brings protection, healing, and luck. Wards against negativity and disaster and helps bind people together. A wreath made with ivy, blackberry, and rowan makes a powerful shield against all evil.

Lavender: Brings love, protection, peace, and sweet dreams. Sew it into the lining of a coat, cape, or jacket to avert the evil eye. It is especially protective for children.

Mint: Attracts money, love, and luck and brings protection to the traveler. Bathe or wash with it to attract needed funds. Keep an open jar of mint in the house to repel vampires, mad dogs, and evil spirits.

Mugwort: Stuff some into your shoes to prevent tiredness all day. Carry the leaves as protection on a journey. Sleep on a pillow of mugwort to enhance your dreams. Drink the tea with yarrow to increase your psychic abilities.

Mullein: Stuff the leaves into pillows and put them under your mattress to ward off nightmares and bad spirits. Carry the herb to bring courage and to strengthen your personal shields.

Nettles: Hang bunches from the door, gateposts, or eaves to keep away unwanted visitors and spirits. (Beware the sting! Wear gloves when you harvest nettles.)

Oregano: Grown near the house, it brings happiness, tranquillity, luck, health, and protection. It aids you in letting go of a loved one and is also used in spells to deepen existing love. Wear it as a crown during sleep to bring psychic dreams. It attracts and magnifies joy. Weave it into a wreath and place it on a grave to ensure that the deceased has a happy next life.

Periwinkle: Also known as "sorcerer's violet." Weave strands of periwinkle into wreaths to protect your home from evil spirits.

Pine: Signifies a willingness to bend, healing, and purification. Pine is the tree of family ties, loving touch, and peace. Use a large pine branch to ritually sweep an area; it will drive away bad energies and bring peace. Or tie a small bundle of pine needles together and burn them in your cauldron. As they burn, pass pinecones through the smoke while thinking of all the good things in your life. Place the cones where you will pass by frequently and be reminded of your blessings.

Purple loosestrife: This plant is considered most powerful when gathered on the Summer Solstice. Place it in the corners of a room to restore harmony and peace and attract protection and peaceful energies to the home. Give it to a friend to help settle an argument.

Red flowers: Plant red flowers of all kinds in the front yard to attract visitors.

Rosemary: Cleansing and purifying. Burn rosemary like incense to repel all negative energies.

Speedwell: Sew it into your jacket, cloak, or coat as a protective charm.

St. John's wort: Dispels melancholy and bad dreams, strengthens health, and brings protection, strength, love, and happiness. Wear it around your neck or hang it in your home as an amulet to drive away evil spirits. St. John's wort is magically protective against "stitch, itch, and cramp": depression, Faery blight, sorcery, ghosts, cow diseases, and bad luck. Smoke it over a Midsummer fire to enhance its magical properties.

Thyme: An herb of grounding, purification, and courage. Carry it to bring energy while walking or when you wish to be praised and admired. To attract love, mix popcorn, sugar, and thyme in a jar (fire, sweetness, and spice). Burn three red candles around the jar while chanting, "Love be here, here to stay, the time is now, light the way." Enhances health and healing, brings sleep, and increases psychic powers. Make a strong tea and use it to wash the floors—like all aromatic herbs, thyme has disinfectant properties. Stuff thyme into every pillow in the house.

Violets: Make a violet flower tea, add milk, and bathe your face in it to make yourself magically beautiful. Especially powerful for children, violets bring protection, peace, and healing. Carry violets to change your fortune and luck.

Wild grasses: Braid your wishes into a talisman of grasses and hang it on the wall. Or tie knots into a long stem of grass while blowing your wish into each knot. Pick a bouquet of grasses with seed heads on them each summer and keep it in the home to attract abundance and prosperity. Use wild grasses to make a corn dolly (see page 145).

Willow: The tree of gentle touch, willingness to bend, healing, poetic genius, new Moon magic, female rites of passage, inspiration, love, love divination, and creativity in general. It is also the tree sacred to poets; in ancient times, bardic harps were made of willow wood.

Yarrow: To see your true love in a dream, place yarrow under your pillow and repeat the following nine times before going to sleep: "Before this night is through, I will see my love, before morning's light, and the Sun's above." Drink yarrow flower tea with mugwort to enhance clairvoyance and psychic powers. Wear it as protection. It is a warrior plant; held in the hand, it brings courage and expels fear. Use it in washes or baths to exorcise evil from the body, places, and things.

8

LUGH OF THE LONG ARM
AND THE BLESSING OF
THE EARLY HARVEST

An Irish Tale for Lúnasa
(August 1)

················· **Key Figures and Terms** ·················

Gods, Goddesses, Spirits, and Magical Beings:

Aonbharr (*IN-bear*)—literally, "froth"; a magical horse. It could travel on land and sea and was swifter than the wind.

Balor (*BAH-lohr*)—better known as Balor of the Evil Eye, king of the Fomorians. He had a huge, poisonous eye that killed anything it gazed upon.

Cethlenn (*KEH-len*)—wife of Balor and mother of Ethlenn.

Ethlenn (*EH-len*)—daughter of Balor and Cethlenn. Her name means "grain."

Failinis (*FAW-ihn-ish*)—a magical greyhound that was invincible in battle, caught every wild beast it hunted, and could magically transform any water it bathed in to wine.

Fomorians (*FOH-mor-ee-uns*)—a race of giants said to have inhabited Ireland long, long ago.

Lugh (*loo*)—a Celtic God of brilliance, intelligence, and skill and king of the Tuatha Dé Danann.

Manannán Mac Lir (*MAH-nah-non MACK leer*)—a sea God

and member of the Tuatha Dé Danann. The first part of his
name, *Manannán,* means "son of the sea." Adding *Mac Lir*
transforms that to "son of the sea God Lir."

Nuada (*NOO-ahd-ah*)—high king of the Tuatha Dé Danann (see
below).

Selkie (*SELL-kee*)—a magical creature that resembles a seal
in the water but can remove its coat and transform into a
human when it comes to shore.

Tailtiu (*TAIL-tee-ew*)—Goddess of the land and foster mother of
Lugh; she is said to give of herself so the people may eat.

Tuatha Dé Danann (*TOO-ah-hah day dah-nen*)—"People of the
Goddess Danu," a race of magical beings or deities said to
have inhabited Ireland long, long ago. Danu is the Celtic
Earth-Mother Goddess.

Irish/Celtic Words to Know:

daidí (*DAH-dee*)—father.

ficheall (*FEE-hal*)—an ancient Celtic board game thought to be
an ancestor of chess and reportedly invented by Lugh.

Fragarach (*FRAH-gah-rach*)—the sword of Nuada, which he
bestowed upon Lugh as a symbol of kingship. Also known
as "The Answerer," the sword would force anyone it was
pointed at to answer questions truthfully. It was also said to
be able to cut through any shield and inflict fatal wounds.

Lúnasa (*LOO-nah-sah*)—the festival of Lugh, celebrating the
first fruits of the harvest.

mamaí (*MAH-mee*)—mother.

shanachie (*SHAH-na-key*)—a traditional teller of tales;
sometimes spelled *seanchaí.*

Sleá of Assal (*sh-LAW of AH-sahl*)—*sleá* means "spear," and
the Spear of Assail was made in the mythical northern
city of Findias and brought into Ireland by the Tuatha Dé
Danann. It is said to have been invincible and unstoppable,
a flaming, fiery spear that hit like lightning and had to have

its head kept submerged in water when it was not in use to keep its flames from growing out of control.

Tir na nÓg (*TEER nah nog*)—literally, "land of youth," meaning the land of the Faeries.

· ·

The festival of Lúnasa derives its name from the classic Irish *Lúghnasadh*. A *nasad* is an assembly, and thus Lúnasa is the "Assembly of Lugh." Lugh is a Celtic God of supreme intelligence, magical skills, and the harvest and also a warrior-king of the mythical Tuatha Dé Danann. This festival celebrates the beginning of the harvest season and also honors Lugh's foster mother, the Earth Goddess Tailtiu. Lúnasa was begun by Lugh as funeral games in her honor.

Tailtiu had cleared the land for the people, allowing them to plant fields and graze flocks, but her efforts exhausted her and she died. While Lúnasa is a celebration of Lugh's victories as king, it is also a memorial to Tailtiu and a way to give thanks for the first fruits of the harvest, which would not have been possible without her sacrifice. It is said that Tailtiu died on August 1. In her honor, Lúnasa is celebrated from the end of July to mid-August. When the Gregorian calendar was adopted in 1782, eleven days were dropped to make the calendar astronomically correct. Thus, Lúnasa rituals may be performed on August 1 (new style) or August 12 (old style).

Lúnasa is celebrated on hilltops, on the tops of mountains, on riverbanks, and by ponds and lakes. Offerings such as fresh butter, flowers, and fruits are left on or beside holy wells, lakes, and waterways. Loaves of bread made with the new grain are shared. Great fairs are held, with athletic, music, dance, and poetry competitions. Debts are settled, weddings or hand-fastings (trial marriages of a year and a day) performed, contracts signed, and new laws declared. It can be a wild, joyful time to thank the Gods for the abundance of the crops and to ask for their blessing in gathering the harvest, which is not yet safely completed.

✳

The old *shanachie* was making his rounds again, and as usual was on his way to the little thatched cottage where Fiona and her family lived. It was now mid-July, high summer, which was always a good time for a tale because the crops had been planted but the harvest had not yet begun.

The days were long at this time of year, and the Sun still shone even after supper was finished and all the dishes were put away. In the evenings, Fiona liked to sit on the little wall in front of the thatched cottage and watch the horses and carts pass by. She always waved at them, whether she recognized the horses and riders or not. This evening she was thrilled to see the shanachie making his way down the lane. Fiona noticed that he was carrying something new this time—a long, shiny stick.

"Hullo!" Fiona cried as she ran to give him a hug. At five years of age, she was so small that she could only reach his legs, but the shanachie bent down to bring himself closer.

"What's that you're carrying?" Fiona asked.

"This? Why, this is my Faery stick. It's made from a blackthorn tree. It brings me luck and protection everywhere I travel!"

Fiona's eyes grew wide and round as copper pennies. The shanachie was always full of surprises. "Have you come to tell us another story?"

"Why yes, I have!" said the shanachie. "It's almost time for the reaping to begin, so I thought I would tell you a story about Lugh, the great God of the Harvest."

You see, the shanachie was one of a long line of storytellers, each the son of a storyteller, trained by his father and his grandfathers before him. Their lineage went all the way back to the ancient Druids. It was the responsibility of the Druids and bards to pass down the old tales because they had so much wisdom hidden in them and were far too precious to be forgotten.

The shanachie entered the house with Fiona dancing at his feet. Mamaí took his cloak and walking stick as Daidí handed him a cool glass of apple cider. Fiona's grandmother led him to his usual seat by the fire, and just as soon as he was settled the neighbors started coming in. When everyone was comfortably seated, the shanachie cleared his throat, took one more sip of cider, and began to spin his tale.

"It was the end of summer, a long, long, long time ago, when the grain was yellow and already ripening in the fields but not yet ready to be cut."

"You mean like now?" asked Fiona, who was seated on the floor gazing up at the shanachie with excitement in her eyes.

"Shhhhh!" said Mamaí, in a loud whisper.

The shanachie continued:

Long, long, long ago, on a high summer evening just like this one, King Balor of the Evil Eye and his wife, Queen Cethlenn, gave birth to a baby girl, whom they named Ethlenn. They were thrilled and very proud, but they were also afraid. A terrible prophecy had been made about the newborn girl, declaring that a child of Ethlenn would one day grow up to kill King Balor!

Now King Balor had to make a very hard decision. Should he allow Ethlenn to live and one day give birth to a child who would be his death? Or should he have Ethlenn killed so he himself could remain safe? Balor thought long and hard about it. It was a very difficult decision to make because the king and queen already loved their baby daughter deeply.

He finally decided what to do. He would seal Ethlenn in a tower of glass where she would want for nothing. She would have a twelve serving women to tend to her every need, and the twelve serving women would be under the strictest orders to never let Ethlenn see a man, or even hear one spoken of. Kept away from all the rest of human society, Ethlenn would never marry, nor bear a child, nor be the cause of the death of her father.

King Balor's plan was carried out, and the tower was erected on Tory Island off the northwest coast of County Donegal, the most remote inhabited island of Ireland. Ethlenn grew healthy and strong and very beautiful, with raven-dark locks, teeth like pearls, and Moon-white skin.

At about the time Ethlenn attained adulthood, her father stole a magical cow. That cow was very large and very beautiful. She had white hair with green spots, and she gave unending streams of milk. She belonged to a Fairy named Cian, of the Tuatha Dé Danann, and he was furious over the loss of that cow!

Cian decided he had to do something about it, so he consulted with a Druidess of *the Tuatha Dé Danann, Bioróg, who advised him to ransom his cow by stealing Balor's most precious possession. Then she magically transported him to Ethlenn's glass tower.**

The moment Cian and Ethlenn set eyes on each other, they fell in love. But Cian couldn't stay with her, because he knew that would cause a war between his own tribe, the Tuatha Dé Danann, and King Balor's tribe, the Fomorians. Cian promised Ethlenn that he would return for her as soon as he was able.

Nine months later, Ethlenn gave birth to triplets, one with hair like spun gold, just like Cian, and two with raven-dark locks, just like Ethlenn. When King Balor heard the news, he flew into a rage and ran to the glass tower to tear the children away from their mother, for he had never forgotten the terrible prophecy that a child of Ethlenn's would kill him.

King Balor wrapped each child in a blanket and then threw all three into the ocean, leaving their fate to the wild waves. But King Balor had no idea that Manannán Mac Lir, the God of the sea, was listening and watching. Taking pity on the innocent newborns, Manannán raised a giant wave that swept the golden-haired child right into Cian's arms. The second child, a raven-haired girl, he transformed into a Selkie, and she was the first of that race. The third child he changed into a Merman by giving him a fish tail, and that is how the first Mermaids were created.

Cian called the golden-haired child Lugh, and he loved the boy above all things because he looked just like Ethlenn, only with golden hair. When Cian went looking for a nursemaid from his tribe to foster his son, a mysterious stranger, who was enveloped by a strange mist as he walked, offered his services. The stranger showed himself to be a great warrior and poet, so Cian found him worthy and handed Lugh over to him.

That mysterious man was none other than Manannán Mac Lir, lord of the sea! He took Lugh to Tailtiu, Goddess of the land, who nursed him.

By the time Lugh grew to be a man, he had been very well trained by his foster parents, and one day Manannán said he was finally ready to find a place at the high king's court. So, Lugh set off to make his way in the world, and when he got to the gates of the high king's court, he immediately asked to be let in.

---

*Cian's name is pronounced *KEE-an,* and it means "ancient." Bioróg's name is pronounced *bih-ROHG,* and it means "rough horsetail" (*Equisetum hyemale*), a type of gritty and tough plant that grows in damp areas.

"Who goes there?" asked the gatekeeper, standing high above on a rampart, looking down.

"I am the greatest warrior in the land!" proclaimed Lugh. "Let me in!"

"Oh, go away," said the gatekeeper. "We already have the finest warriors at this court, and we certainly don't need you!" (The gatekeeper thought that Lugh was being rather cheeky and wanted to put him in his place.)

"I am also the finest goldsmith you will ever meet!" Lugh declared. "Let me in!"

"We already have the greatest jewelers and blacksmiths and artists of all kinds within these walls. Go away! We don't need you," the gatekeeper replied.

"Well, I am also the greatest healer and herbalist in the land. I can cure any sickness or injury!" said Lugh.

"We already have the most skillful wise women and cunning men you will ever meet," said the gatekeeper. "So, be gone!"

"I am the best bard and the most brilliant poet!" said Lugh. "I deserve a place at the high court, so let me in!"

Now the gatekeeper was really getting impatient. He had never heard such an insistent, boastful, persistent youth. "We already have the wisest Druids, poets, and sages at this court. We don't need you! So please go away!" he declared firmly.

But Lugh kept right on, describing his talents as a magician, harpist, judge, historian, cupbearer, sportsman, master of ficheall, and more. But the gatekeeper wouldn't budge, and the great oaken door remained firmly bolted.

Finally, when Lugh could not think of one more talent to boast of, he asked, "Do you have anyone in this court who can do all those things?"

Now that stumped the gatekeeper. He was very quiet for a moment, because he was thinking. At last he replied, "Alright, you win. We do not have anyone here who is skilled in every art." And slowly the heavy oaken gates parted and Lugh was let in.

Lugh really was exactly as brilliant as he had claimed, and eventually the high king of the Tuatha de Danann, Nuada, passed his crown to him, because Lugh was the worthiest champion in all the kingdoms.

One day Balor of the Evil Eye, Lugh's own grandfather, arrived with his warriors to attack the very fort where Lugh had been made king. Lugh, who was now known as Lugh of the Long Arm because he could throw a spear so far and so accurately, rode out to defend the fort.

There at the front of the fray was King Balor, a fearful sight, with one red eye that shone from his forehead casting a burning, deadly blaze onto his foes. Every warrior in the field was instantly struck dead by that terrible light, except Lugh.

Lugh was armed with his enchanted spear, the Sleá of Assal, which struck like lightning and was unbeatable in battle. He also carried his mighty slingshot, and his sword, Fragrarach, which would force anyone it was pointed at to answer questions truthfully. He rode upon his mystical horse, Aonbharr of the Flowing Mane, gifted to him by Manannán, who could gallop over both land and sea, and beside him ran his magical greyhound, Failinis, who was invincible in battle, always caught its prey, and could change water into wine. Lugh simply waited for his grandfather to blink, and then he slung a great stone from his slingshot right into the center of Balor's fearful eye, killing him instantly. And thus, the old prophecy was fulfilled.

Balor, of course, was king of the Fomorians. With Balor's death, Lugh became the ruler of the Tuatha Dé Danann and the Fomorians, too!

Lugh created the festival of Lúnasa in part to celebrate his victory over King Balor and the Fomorians and also to honor Tailtiu, his foster mother. After his own death, Lugh went to dwell in Tír na nÓg, the land of the Faeries, but he always comes back when he is needed. And this is why folk call on Lugh when they need strength and inspiration to perform any difficult task.

"You mean like getting the whole harvest in?" Fiona blurted out, because she just couldn't keep quiet a minute longer.

"Exactly," the shanachie said.

The old storyteller had finished his tale. He wiped his forehead with a handkerchief from his pocket and took a long sip of cider. He had put all of his energy and enthusiasm into telling that story because he never wanted to disappoint the great God Lugh nor Manannán Mac Lir, whom he felt sure must be listening.

That night, after Fiona was tucked in and kissed goodnight by Mamaí, she lay awake imagining what it would be like to live in a tower of glass, like Ethlenn did, and be able to lie in bed and look up to see the Moon and stars through the walls and the ceiling. And then she fell into a deep, dreaming sleep.*

THE LÚNASA FEAST
....

Bilberries (Vaccinium myrtillus) become ripe at about the same time as Lúnasa, and it is said that if the bilberries are plentiful, so will the harvest be. Many of the dishes at a Lúnasa feast feature bilberries, including bilberry pies, cakes, tarts, syrups, and jams. Baskets of the berries might decorate the holiday table. (Bilberries are very similar to blueberries, in case you were wondering. You can substitute blueberries for bilberries in any recipe.)

The focus of the feast is the beginning of the harvest, so fresh baked goods, especially loaves of bread made from the new grain, are also appropriate on the table, as are any other dishes made from the early harvest. It is very good luck to harvest new potatoes at Lúnasa (but very bad luck to dig them up before that), so be sure to include a dish of new potatoes with fresh butter, too. You can make some new butter yourself (see page 53 for the recipe)!

🍃 BILBERRY SCONES 🍃

4 cups cake flour, plus extra as needed for kneading

3 teaspoons non-aluminum baking powder

½ teaspoon sea salt

4 ounces (1 stick) butter

½ cup sugar, plus 2 tablespoons to sprinkle on top

1½ cups fresh or frozen bilberries or blueberries (if frozen, thaw and drain them)

---

*This tale is the Irish version of the birth of Lugh. You may be wondering what happened to Ethlenn after her babies were abducted. The birth of Lleu (Lugh) in the Welsh mythos is a quite similar tale. In that account, Lleu's mother, Aranrhod, a sky Goddess whose name means "silver wheel," seems to prefer to stay in her tower, away from her meddling male relatives!

    2 large eggs

    ¾ cup milk (cow, soy, almond, cashew, coconut, rice, oat,
        hemp, or flax)

Preheat the oven to 425°F. Grease a baking tray.

Sift the flour, baking powder, and salt into a large bowl.

Cut the butter into 1-inch pieces and drop them into the flour mixture. Use two knives to cut the butter pieces into the flour, or rub them in using your fingers, until the mixture resembles fine breadcrumbs.

Add the sugar and mix it in.

Add the berries and stir gently to disperse them throughout the flour mixture.

In a separate bowl or pitcher, whisk the eggs and milk together.

Make a well in the middle of the dry ingredients and pour in most of the liquid. Reserve about ¼ cup of the liquid mixture to brush on top of the unbaked scones.

Using a large spoon or your hand, mix the wet and dry ingredients together to form a soft-but-not-too-sticky dough. Add some more flour if the dough sticks to the sides of the bowl. Add a little of the egg and milk mixture if the dough is too dry and won't come together. Handle the dough gently to avoid bursting the berries.

Turn the dough out onto a lightly floured surface. Sprinkle with a little more flour. Knead the dough lightly.

Using your hands or a rolling pin (or glass bottle), flatten the dough into a large round disk about 1½ inches thick.

Use a biscuit cutter or an upside-down drinking glass to cut out round shapes.

Place the rounds of dough on the greased baking tray.

Brush the top of the rounds with the reserved egg and milk mixture.

Sprinkle the top of each round with a little sugar.

Bake at 425°F for 10 minutes. Then reduce the heat to 400°F and bake for another 15 to 20 minutes, until the tops are slightly golden.

Remove from the oven and let cool on a wire rack for 10 minutes.

Enjoy these scones with butter, clotted cream, and/or jam or jelly. They are delicious served slightly warm and fresh from the oven.

_____

This recipe is adapted from Mairead Geary, "Blueberry Scones," Irish American Mom (website), June 21, 2014.

🍂 BILBERRY PIE 🍃

5 cups fresh or frozen bilberries or blueberries (if frozen, thaw and drain them)

1 tablespoon lemon juice

1 (15-ounce) package prepared pie crust (with two crusts)

1 cup sugar, plus 1 teaspoon for sprinkling on top

½ cup all-purpose flour, plus extra for rolling out the crust

⅛ teaspoon sea salt

½ teaspoon ground cinnamon

2 tablespoons butter, cut into small pieces

1 large egg, lightly beaten

1 teaspoon sugar

Preheat the oven to 400°F.

Sprinkle the berries with the lemon juice and set aside.

Lay one pastry crust in a 9-inch pie plate, draping its edges over the rim of the dish.

Combine 1 cup of sugar with the flour, salt, and cinnamon in a bowl and mix well.

Add the sugar mixture to the berries and toss to combine.

Pour the berry mixture into the pie plate. Scatter the pieces of butter over the filling.

Unfold the second pie crust and lay it on a lightly floured surface. Roll it gently with a rolling pin or a glass bottle to remove any creases in the pastry.

Lay the crust over the filling. Seal and crimp the edges of the two crusts with your fingers or a fork.

Cut a few slits in the top of the crust to allow steam to escape.

Brush the top of the pie with the beaten egg, and sprinkle with the remaining 1 teaspoon of sugar.

Bake for about 35 minutes, or until golden on top. Cover the edges of the pie with aluminum foil to prevent overbrowning, if necessary.

Let cool, then slice and eat!

This recipe is adapted from Michael Gilligan, "Lughnasa Recipes, Rituals, Traditions and Symbols for the Ancient Celtic Festival," IrishCentral (website), August 6, 2021.

· · · · · · · · · · · · · · ·   **The Nicknames of Lugh**   · · · · · · · · · · · · · · ·

The great God Lugh was very popular among the ancient Celts. The only other deity who might have been as popular was Brighid (and you can read all about her in chapter 4). As you probably know, when someone is very popular, people like to give them nicknames. Lugh had many such names. Following are a few of them:

Lugh Lámh Fhada—"Lugh of the Long Arm," due to the length of his battle spear and how far he could throw it

Lugh Lonnbhéimneach—"Lugh, Fierce Striker"

Lugh Ildánach—"Lugh, Skilled in Many Arts"

Lugh Samhaildánach—"Lugh, Equally Skilled in All the Arts"

Lugh Macnia—"Lugh, Youthful Warrior-Hero"

Lugh Conmac—"Lugh, Hound Son," because Lugh's son was the hero Cú Chulainn, the Hound of Ulster (who is also believed by many to have been the reincarnation of Lugh)

Lugh Ollamh Éireann—"Lugh, Chief Poet of Ireland"

· ·

❋

Games and Competitions for Your Lúnasa Celebration

In ancient times, Lúnasa was all about games and competitions: wrestling, spear throwing, running, high jumping, long jumping, horse racing, hurling, weight throwing, staff fighting, arm wrestling, ball throwing, archery, and tug-of-war. Poets even competed for the title of Chief Poet. In modern times, you may also find "Bonnie Baby" competitions, dog shows, judging of crafts, and the like.

Here are some fun, traditional games that you can incorporate into your own Lúnasa celebration. You will notice that quite a few of them involve horseshoes. As solar animals, horses are sacred to the celebration of Lúnasa and the first fruits of the harvest. Part of the ritual celebration involves driving horses through water, bringing together fire and water (the two basic building blocks of creation, according to the ancient Celts), and creating the greatest potential for magic.

Hood Man Blind (or Blind Man's Bluff)

This game comes from medieval times. The "hood man" wears a hood (a cloth sack or pillowcase will do), which is tied around their neck with a bandana or soft ribbon. The other players strike at the hood man with their own hoods until he catches and names one of them. That person becomes the next hood man.

Horseshoe Pitching

This ancient game was once played by Roman soldiers. Horseshoes are thrown at a stake, and points are awarded to the person who gets their shoe closest to or around the stake.

Two or three people can compete against each other as individual players. A group of four can divide into two teams of two people. Men pitch from a distance of forty feet, and women and children from thirty feet.

Each player throws two shoes, underhanded, for a predetermined number of turns. You might take up to twenty-five turns.

3 points	The shoe encircles the stake without touching it. This throw is called a *ringer.*
1 point	The shoe leans against the stake. This throw is called a *leaner.*
1 point	The shoe lands within six inches of the stake.

Kayles

Eight conical cones of wood (or cardboard), each about six inches tall, are placed inside a chalk circle. Contestants throw a stick at them from about ten feet away. Every contestant gets three tries, and whoever knocks over the most cones wins.

King of the Hill

Find a hill. The first person to get to the top wins.

Lammas

This game comes from Scotland. Each competitor holds a straw between their chin and chest. The winner is the person who can recite this rhyme the most times without dropping the straw:

> *I bought a beard at Lammas Fair,*[*]
> *It's a' awa' but ae hair-wag, beardiewag!*

Lifting Sticks

Two people sit on the floor facing each other, with their legs stretched out and the soles of their feet touching. A broom or long stick is laid over their feet and gripped at each end by the competitors. Each pulls at the broom, trying to lift their opponent off the floor a few inches without bending a leg. The soles of their feet must remain in contact at all times. The moment one person's derriere leaves the floor, the other person wins.

Lift the Horseshoe

A horseshoe is placed three inches away from a wall. The contestant stands three feet from the wall and must pick up the horseshoe without bending a knee or placing a hand on the wall or the floor.

---

[*]In the Christian era, people brought loaves of bread made with the new grain to be blessed at church. Thus, Lúnasa is sometimes also known as Lammas ("Loaf Mass").

Rhibo

This is an old Welsh harvest game. Three pairs of people face each other, with each pair holding hands. A person lies down across their hands, and the paired people toss that person into the air repeatedly, mimicking the act of winnowing wheat. You can also play this game as a blanket toss.

Robins Alight

Place a lit candle inside an open jar and pass it quickly from person to person. The person holding the candle when the flame goes out must perform a task or pay a fine (these should be decided beforehand).

Slap Hands

A medieval game in which a blindfolded player kneels with their hands behind their back. The other players take turns tapping the hands of the kneeling person. Each time the kneeling player tries to guess who struck them. Once they guess correctly, that person takes their place.

Stick Jumping

Each competitor holds the ends of a four-foot-long stick and tries to jump over it without letting go.

"Wife" Carrying

In this race, each contestant runs with their "wife"—which can be any other person—on their back, thrown over their shoulder, or piggyback style. The contestants should be evenly matched, and the race is about a hundred yards in distance.

❋

Perform a Play

The Celtic God Crom Dubh (pronounced *crumb dove*), "dark crooked one," is said to live in the underworld of the Sidhe all winter, spends the spring and summer nurturing the crops, and then guards them as his own personal treasure. This play, which can be performed as part of a ritual or as a fun activity, pits Lugh against Crom Dubh. The exact details of the storyline are up to the play participants, but Lugh, a tall, straight, shining, Sun-like figure, must overcome Crom Dubh so that humanity can have the crops to eat.

Alternatively, Lugh may compete against a dragon, who represents the powerful Earth energies that guard the treasures of nature and the soil. Lugh triumphs in the end, of course, symbolizing humankind's ability to wrest nourishment and sustenance from the land by using intelligence, determination, and skill.

❋

Other Activities at Lúnasa

It is very important to make offerings to the Faeries and Land Spirits at this time in thanks for their work in growing the crops and other plants. The first "fruits" from the garden—vegetables, flowers, herbs, roots, and berries—can be left as a gift for the Land Spirits and Faeries on top of a hill or mountain.

You can also make an offering to Tailtiu, foster mother of Lugh, who can be understood as the Earth Mother who nourishes us all. It is appropriate to leave a portion of the first harvest for her, the Faeries, and Land Spirits somewhere on the ground, on top of a rock, in a wild part of the garden, by a water source, under a special tree, or any other sacred place. Examples might be a few ripe rose hips, the first tomato, a bunch of fresh herbs, an ear of corn, a new potato, a ripe melon, some flowers from the garden, or a few stalks of grain.

Traditionally, the first sheaf of grain cut from a field is carried to a hilltop or mountaintop, dedicated to Lugh, and buried with thanks.

❋

Visit Holy Wells

Walk sunwise (clockwise) around a holy well three or nine times, then leave an offering, such as a coin or a fresh flower. Take a strip of rag or ribbon and dip it into the water of the well, then press it against any part of you that is ailing. Tie the rag to a tree that overhangs the well. As the cloth rots away, so will your troubles.*

If there is no holy well in your area, you can always make your own. I have one in the forest behind my house, dedicated to Brighid. Druids who come to my home have made offerings there for more than thirty years. It is a natural forest pool that is fed by a stream behind the house. Over the years we have dug it out and lined it with rocks. When the well fills after a rainstorm, the water spills over the rocks and makes a sound like a tiny waterfall, which is very magical!

---

*In Ireland, a tree like this would be known as a "rag tree." In Scotland, the cloths tied to a rag tree are called *clooties,* and the well that the tree hangs over is called a "clootie well."

9

THE SPIRIT OF THE GRAIN
AND THE SPIRITS OF THE SEA

*A Scottish Tale for the Fall Equinox
(September 21/22/23/24)*

················ **Key Figures and Terms** ················

Gods, Goddesses, Spirits, and Magical Beings:

Cailleach (*KAHL-yuk*)—the Goddess of winter and the land.

Mither o' the Sea (*MIH-ther*)—literally, "Mother of the Sea," the Goddess of the ocean.

Nuckelavee (*NUH-kul-aee-vee*)—a demon or Faery horse that frequents the seashore.

Teran (*TEAR-ran*)—God of the Sea. The name comes from the Norse *tyrren,* meaning "furious anger" or "irritability."

Gaelic and Other Words to Know:

broonie (*BROO-nee*)—a sweet oatmeal gingerbread. The word *broonie* comes from the Old Norse *bruni,* meaning a thick bannock. *Broonie* is also the name of the king of the Trows (a race of Trolls) in Orkney legend and the Scottish name for a Brownie!

clapshaw (*CLAP-shaw*)—a dish of mashed potatoes and yellow turnips mixed with milk, butter, and chives.

faether (*FEH-ther*)—father.

Gore Vellye (*goar VAIL-yuh*)—the Fall Equinox, when the lengths of the day and night are even.

mither (*MIH-ther*)—mother.

This story has a little bit of America in it and a little bit of Orkney in it. Orkney is at the very northern tip of Scotland; it is a collection of seventy islands that once belonged to the king of Norway but are now part of Scotland. Everyone who lives in Orkney lives close to the sea, so Lorna's family naturally settled close to the seashore when they came to America.

Because the sea is so important to them for their livelihood, the people of Orkney pay very close attention to what the ocean is doing and the creatures that dwell in it. They spin tales of Mermaids and of the great sea battles between the ruler of summer, Mither o' the Sea, and the ruler of the winter waves, Teran. They also know how to practice a bit of protective magic such as tossing a sprig of juniper or a piece of broonie into the fire to protect the house from evil and storms.

Fall Equinox is the time when the seas become rough as the winter gales set in. It is also the middle of the harvest, when day and night are of equal length, and the family pauses the harvest to have a feast in honor of the occasion.

✴

Lorna lived in New England on a farm near the sea, and fall was her favorite season. This year she was in fourth grade and just old enough to walk to and from school by herself. She loved the start of the school year because it meant she finally got to see her friends again after a long summer. There was so much to share and to talk about!

Every day on the way to school, she passed by a row of ancient maple trees planted in a line along the roadside. Each spring, she, her parents, and her grandma Torrie hung metal buckets on the trees to collect fresh sap to boil down for syrup.

Now that it was almost the Fall Equinox, the maples were starting to turn color. Vivid oranges and reds were already mixing in with the green of the leaves. Purple, pink, and white asters bloomed along the roadside and in her mother's garden, and at the bottom of the garden, the small orchard of apples and crab apples was brightly hung with yellow and red fruits. Mither and Grandma Torrie had been busy all week canning apple butter and jelly and preserving spiced apple slices to serve at Thanksgiving and Christmas dinners.

The scent of grapes was in the air; wild fox grapes and Concord grapes had spread in dense mats from tree to tree along the edge of the forest. The fox grapes could not be eaten until after the first frost, but Mither and Grandma Torrie had been picking Concord grapes for weeks to make grape jelly, juice, and pie. There were still some blackberries in the hedges if you looked carefully, but they were far and few between because the birds had already picked off the best ones.

Faether's wheat field was ripe and tall and ready to be harvested, so long as the weather stayed fine. The golden stalks waved and rippled in the wind as if in greeting when Lorna walked by. Dry yellow corn stalks rustled on the opposite side of the lane as V-shaped flocks of geese flew overhead, honking to keep each other in line.

Grandma Torrie came from a place called Orkney in the northernmost islands of Scotland. She was always passing down stories from her girlhood to Lorna. "Because you have to know where you come from, even if you have never been there," she would say.

That afternoon, after Lorna had walked home from school and had a snack of milk and oatmeal raisin cookies, Grandma Torrie asked if she would like to go for a walk. "I have been working in the kitchen all day, and it would be nice to spend some time outside. But don't forget to put on a jacket. The breeze off the ocean is getting colder every day!"

"Oh Grandma," Lorna replied, "I will, and I hope you will tell me another story about when you were a girl!" That was the best thing about having a grandma—you could always hear a story about the olden times.

Soon they were walking down the lane that Lorna took to get to school, and Grandma Torrie saw the field of waving wheat. "Do you know why it waves like that?" she asked.

Lorna studied the field for a few moments. It looked as if something was swimming through the grain. "Is it the wind that makes it ripple that way?" she asked.

"Actually," Grandma Torrie replied, "it's the spirit of the grain. It's a living force that moves through the field as it grows, quickening the ripening stalks."

"What does it look like? I can't see it!" said Lorna.

"Well, if you ask me, it looks like a wolf, or maybe a dog," Grandma Torrie replied. "Something that lives near the house but is still wild. Though some say it is a Spirit Goat. Back in Orkney, when the harvest was done a straw dog or straw goat was made from the last sheaf cut by each farmer and then passed on to another farmer who was still threshing. That farmer would pass it on yet again—it was very bad luck to be the last farmer holding the straw goat!"

"I bet that made the farmers work faster!" Lorna said.

"Exactly!" said Grandma Torrie. "With the winter coming on, everyone had to work quickly to get the harvest in."

As they kept walking, they came to a blackberry patch with just a few fat, juicy berries still clinging to the brambles.

"Ooh! Let's pick some of those!" cried Lorna.

"Oh, no, better not," Grandma Torrie said. "Didn't we have a hard frost last week? Once that happens all the berries belong to the Faeries, and it is bad luck to even touch them!"

"I didn't know that," Lorna replied. It seemed like she learned something new every day. And now she was feeling a little sad, too, because that meant there would be no more blackberries until next summer—a whole year away!

"No reason to look so sad," said Grandma Torrie. "Your mother and I have been canning blackberries and making syrup and jams with them all week. And guess what we are having for dessert tonight?"

"Blackberries?" Lorna asked.

"Blackberry pie!" said Grandma Torrie.

The next day, when Lorna came home from school, Grandma Torrie was already waiting at the door with a basket on her arm. "Come with me," she said mysteriously, offering Lorna her arm.

"Where are we going now?" asked Lorna. Grandma Torrie always found exciting things to do.

"Just drop your books and follow me!" she replied.

And off they went, arm in arm, down to the wheat field. When they got there, the whole field was bare! There was nothing left but stubble, and crows were patrolling the rows, searching for fallen grains. But in the far distance Lorna could see a small bound sheaf of wheat still standing.

"That's the Cailleach, the Old Woman—we left her just for you so you can make a corn dolly for the winter!"

"Ooh," said Lorna, already running toward the sheaf of wheat. Grandma Torrie followed with her basket. When she got to the sheaf, she took out some scissors and handed them to Lorna so she could cut the stalks of grain.

"Be sure you cut close to the ground!" said Grandma Torrie. "You need the stalks to be long so you can make a proper doll! That little doll has to hold the spirit of the grain until next spring and carry the luck of the harvest from this year to the next. She will sit in the place of honor on the mantel all winter, and we will bury her in this field next spring, when Faether does the planting."

Lorna carefully cut each stalk and laid them in a neat bundle on the ground.

"Here is some string to tie them up," said Grandma Torrie, pulling brown twine from her basket. "And now that we have taken what we needed from the field, what do you think we should do next?"

"Should we give something back?" asked Lorna.

"You are a very smart girl, and well trained by your parents," replied Grandma Torrie, reaching into her basket again and pulling out a small sack that was filled with birdseed. "Take these seeds and scatter them as a gift to the birds. By giving something back, we will bring good luck to the farm."

Lorna scattered the seeds along the empty rows and stubble so the hungry birds would have something good to eat.

"Now, let's get back home for our Gore Vellye celebration and supper!" Grandma Torrie said. "And if you are extra good and *very* helpful, I might even sit by the fire and tell you how Mermaids were created and other magical things!" she added with a wink.

"Oh yes!" said Lorna, clapping her hands. There was nothing she liked more than a storytelling session with Grandma by the fire.

That night the family had a very special supper. Before they began eating, Faether spoke about the significance of the day: "On the day of the Equinox, it's not quite dark and it's not quite light. Today the day was exactly as long as the night, but by tomorrow the night will be just a few minutes longer than the day. And so it will continue until we slide into the darkest days of winter! Right now, we are still in the middle of the harvest season, which is why we stop for a moment to give thanks. The harvest won't be completely in until Samhain, when everything is safely stored in the barn and kitchen cupboards. Then we will celebrate again!"

"But the wheat field is completely bare now," said Lorna. "I thought you had finished bringing it all in."

"Yes, we did," said Mither, "but we still have more harvesting to come—the sheep and the cows that we can't afford to feed all winter will be harvested. And so will the geese."

That all made sense to Lorna, even if it made her a little sad.

It was a fine spread—Grandma Torrie made sure of that, preparing all the dishes her family had enjoyed when she was a girl living in Orkney. There was *clapshaw* (mashed potatoes and yellow turnips), a fat roasted goose, and freshly baked sourdough bread into which Mither had put a little of each of the grains grown on the farm—wheat, barley, and rye. There were new carrots, freshly dug, new wine made from the Concord grapes that grew on the land, and freshly pressed grape juice for Lorna. For dessert there was a gingerbread *broonie* with a scoop of whipped cream on the side, and a magnificent blackberry pie, made with the very last berries of the year.

Before they ate, everyone listed three things they were grateful for and then named a new project that they wanted to begin in the winter. Then they dug in.

"Pay attention to the color of the goose bones!" declared Grandma Torrie while everyone else was chewing. "If they are brown, that means a mild winter is coming, but if the bones are white like snow and ice, it means a harsh winter lies ahead." The bones were brown, and everyone gave a sigh of relief.

When the meal was done, they went to the parlor, where Faether lit the fire and Grandma Torrie sprinkled dried juniper on the flames, saying, "The smoke of this burning juniper will start the season right!"

Then everyone sat back on a comfortable pillow, sofa, or chair and prepared to listen as Grandma spun her tales.

"In the land where I am from—and you are, too, though you have never been there—we live close by the sea."

"So do we!" said Lorna. "We can see the ocean just by standing on the high wall behind the barn!"

"Just so," said Grandma Torrie. "And that is why I am going to tell you the lore of the sea that I learned when I was exactly your age, back in Orkney. We always paid close attention to the ocean, because our faethers mostly made their living as fishermen. Everyone wanted to know what the weather would be and how to prepare for it. It was a matter of life and death for us. The most important spirits of the ocean were called Teran and Mither o' the Sea. Sea Mither and Teran are invisible to us humans, but you can follow their activities quite clearly as the seasons change."

"What does Teran look like?" Lorna asked.

"He is a huge sea monster with cold eyes that never blink," said Faether.

"You mean like a shark?" Lorna asked. She had seen sharks brought in by fishermen and some that were stranded on the beach.

"Quite so!" said Grandma Torrie. "He also has huge, twining tentacles and big barnacle-crusted flippers that he uses to churn the sea into giant waves. If a sudden summer storm rises up, that's him thrashing about, trying to escape the powers of Mither o' the Sea.

She continued, "In the springtime, at the time of the Equinox, Sea Mither battles with Teran, and she always wins. She sends him deep under the waves and holds him captive. But that takes all her strength, and by the Fall Equinox she is quite exhausted and loses her grip. Then Teran rises from the ocean floor once more and rules all winter, until Mither o' the Sea can get her strength back at the Spring Equinox.

"And so," Grandma Torrie told them, "every Equinox, spring and fall, they battle for weeks. You always know when it is happening because there are gales, high winds, dark skies, howling blizzards, huge waves, and cold waters that boil and churn.

"But Sea Mither always hears the cries of drowning people and of people crying on the shore—anyone who is starving, sick, or cold—even in the winter when her powers are weakest," she said. "So, you can call on her any time you need protection. But her powers are at their peak in summer, of course. She is the one who repairs and replenishes the land after it is ravished by Teran's freezing winter reign. She is the one who gives the sea creatures the strength to have their babies, warms the oceans, and sends the gentle sea breezes. She keeps Teran and the other dark sea creatures in check!"

Grandma Torrie reached over to her dessert plate, took a small piece of broonie, and threw it into the fire. "To keep evil forces away," she explained, adding, "and now it's time for bed. Sweet dreams and good night!"

🍃 BROONIE (OATMEAL GINGERBREAD) 🍃

Serve your broonie with whipped cream or vanilla ice cream on the side, or have it with butter, jam, or yogurt for breakfast.

1½ cups old-fashioned rolled oats

1 cup whole-wheat flour

1 cup all-purpose flour

½ cup packed brown sugar

1½ teaspoons baking powder

1½ teaspoons ground ginger

½ teaspoon sea salt

½ cup (1 stick) unsalted butter

3 large eggs

1 cup buttermilk

¼ cup molasses

½ cup diced candied ginger

½ cup raisins, optional

Preheat the oven to 350°F. Grease an 8½- by 4½-inch loaf pan.

Combine the oats, flours, sugar, baking powder, ginger, and salt in a large bowl and mix well.

Cut the butter into 1-inch pieces and drop them into the flour mixture. Use two knives to cut the butter pieces into the flour mixture, or rub them in using your fingers, until the mixture resembles coarse cornmeal or sand.

Combine the eggs, buttermilk, and molasses in a second bowl and mix well.

Add the liquid mixture to the dry mixutre, stirring until the batter is evenly moistened.

Stir in the candied ginger and the raisins, if you're using them.

Pour the batter into the prepared pan.

Bake for 65 to 70 minutes, until a skewer or knife inserted in the center comes out clean.

Remove from the oven and let cool on a rack.

Once the loaf is cool, turn it out of the pan, wrap it well, and let it sit overnight before slicing.

This recipe is adapted from "Broonie," King Arthur Baking Company (website), accessed June 7, 2020.

✻

Make a Corn Dolly

A corn dolly carries the luck of the harvest from one year to the next. Make one from the first or last sheaf of grain of a newly harvested field, following the instructions for making a Brídeóg on page 56. If you don't have access to a fresh sheaf of grain, craft stores sell bunches of dried wheat, and you can use them. Or see if you can harvest tall, wild grasses from a field.

At the next Spring Equinox, or at the start of the planting season where you live, bury the corn dolly in the field. Alternatively, the youngest girl of the house can carry the corn dolly to the highest point in the local area and leave it there as an offering of thanks. Or hang it over the barn door. Then sprinkle the corn dolly with water to ensure enough rain for the crops to come.

❋

Make an Equinox Altar

You can make an Equinox altar somewhere in the house or in a covered place outside. Remember that Fall Equinox is the *middle* of the harvest. The harvest is not quite finished and there are still things to do. It is nice to put a few samples of what you are harvesting now on the altar. That could be vegetables, herbs or flowers if you have a garden, or images of things that you are achieving in your life at this time, as well as images of the things you want to dream into your life in future.

As you have seen from the story above, Fall Equinox is a time of transition when the oceans churn and boil. A few seashells, a statue of a porpoise or a starfish, and some blue sparkly cloth will evoke the oceans at the change of season. And a Mermaid or Merman can represent the creatures of the ocean, seen and unseen.

The Fall Equinox altar is a place to give thanks for what has been accomplished in the light half of the year and to set your intention for what you wish to accomplish in the dark half of the year.

- Place blue and green cloth and stones on the altar to symbolize the world under the waves.
- Look for things that are unique to the fall, such as pinecones, colorful leaves, seasonal flowers, and freshly fallen nuts, and use them to decorate the altar.
- Place images or little statues of Mermen and Mermaids on the altar, along with a bowl of seawater or saltwater.
- Add pictures or little statues of water animals, such as seals, swans, seagulls, pelicans, otters, fish, dolphins, and whales.
- Place some seashells on the altar.
- Put small bowls of freshly gathered crops—berries, grapes, grains, nuts, apples, or any other seasonal items—on the altar to symbolize the bounty of the land.

An Equinox altar with symbols of autumn as well as the sea.
Photo by Meghan MacLean.

➻ Put written notes on the altar offering thanks for all you have been given this year and identifying anything that would be a seed for future projects and personal growth. (If the altar is outside, place these notes in jars with lids to protect them from the elements.)

--- ❋ ---

Other Fall Equinox Projects

Store fresh produce and herbs for the winter by drying, canning, pickling, and freezing.

Make jams, jellies, and pies from fruits that are ripe at this time.

Make gingerbread creatures—horses, geese, Mermen, Mermaids, and any other symbols of the season.

Make breads and cakes using small bits of many different grains (cornmeal, wheat flour, rye flour, barley flour, and so on) and any berries that are in season (cranberries, blackberries, and so on) to celebrate the harvest.

Bring a basket of fresh vegetables from the garden to a local food bank to feed those in need.

Bake a cake and offer a piece to the fire to appease any evil forces and to ward off bad luck.

Plant a tree. The Fall Equinox is the very best time to do that!

Dig new carrots and tie them in bunches with red ribbons or thread. Give the bunches to friends, sweethearts, and neighbors.

Leave offerings of berries, fruits, flowers, herbs, and nuts outside for the Land Spirits.

In Fall Is the Harvest

In Fall is the harvest.

The pumpkins are fat,
The leaves are falling,
What do you think of that?

In Fall we get apples,
Donuts, and cider,
As wind blows the leaves
Higher and higher!

The cornstalks are yellow
And dried in the Sun.

Raking leaves into piles
Means jumping and fun!

Soon will be Halloween
With goblins and ghosts.

Then comes Thanksgiving
And big turkey roasts.

We give thanks for the harvest
And all that it brings.

Warmth, love, and family
Make our hearts sing!

✹

And the Wheel of the Year begins anew, when the next Samhain rolls around!

INDEX OF RECIPES